GW01090262

THE IMITATION OF CHRIST

Thomas à Kempis

with *The Life of Thomas à Kempis*
By Carl Ullmann

Translated by John Payne
Introduction by Thomas Chalmers
Edited by Howard Malcom

GLH PUBLISHING
Louisville, Kentucky

Sourced from *The Imitation of Christ*.
Gould and Lincoln: Boston, 1861.

GLH Publishing Reprint, 2016
ISBN-13: 978-1-941129-29-6

CONTENTS

PREFACE.

THE CHRISTIAN'S PATTERN, by Thomas A Kempis, has for more than three hundred years been esteemed one of the best practical religious books in existence; and has gone through repeated editions, not only in the original Latin, but in every European language. Because, however, the author, a popish monk, intermingled his thoughts of purgatory, good works, penance, saints, celibacy, a recluse life, etc., in almost every chapter, the work has been justly denied a general circulation among Protestants. A pastor could scarcely lend or recommend it to his parishioners, or must express such reservations as destroyed the confidence and comfort of the reader.

To remedy this disadvantage, Dean Stanhope published a new version, avowing, not only that he translated from the Latin of Castalio, which is greatly altered from the original, but that he had frequently departed from Castalio, abridging, altering and even changing, both language and thoughts at pleasure. Indeed, he declares that his desire was "not so much to acquaint Englishmen with what Kempis thought, as to convey those thoughts, with some degree of that sprightliness and affectionate warmth which the original composer at first felt from them." With Stanhope's edition, as might have been expected, the public were never satisfied, and it has been seldom printed.

With the same desire to divest this invaluable treatise of its improprieties, Wesley translated and greatly abridged it. But he not only omitted much matter as unexceptionable and valuable as that which he retained, but by dividing the whole into separate sentences or paragraphs, like proverbs, utterly destroyed the connection and beauty of the work, and of course greatly impaired the interest of the reader. Notwithstanding these serious objections, the book has been useful, and in some degree popular, particularly among Mr. Wesley's followers.

The best translation within the editor's knowledge is that of Payne, of which many editions have been printed in England and several in this country. Though not servilely literal, he is generally as exact as is consistent with good English; and in reading his version, we enjoy the pleasure of knowing that we have not only the genuine sentiments, but the very diction of the author. Mr. Payne translated from the celebrated edition in Latin of M. Valart, at Paris; which was formed on a laborious collation of manuscripts and old printed copies, and thus purified from more than six hundred errors. Mr. P., however, in adhering to his author has retained, of course, all his sectarian peculiarities, and in this respect lies under insurmountable disadvantages as to the utility of his book in this country.

The present edition is a reprint from Payne, collated with an ancient Latin copy;[1] and is no further abridged than by omitting the exclusive sentiments of a Catholic recluse, and some occasional redundances of style. The language, wherever it seemed susceptible of improvement, either as to elegance or brevity,

---

1   Contained in an edition of his whole works, published at Antwerp by Henry Sommalius, A.D. 1600.

has been modernized; and where he seemed to have missed the precise meaning, or not to have expressed the force of the original, the passages have been entirely rewritten. To prevent the too frequent occurrence of breaks in the text, chapters on similar points have in some instances been conjoined. The whole revision has been performed with the most scrupulous care and diligence. The editor has retained no sentiment which it was thought could offend the most scrupulous Protestant ear; and, on the other hand, has conscientiously avoided making the author speak sentiments not contained in the text. He felt himself at full liberty to expunge, but not authorized to add or alter.

That this book does not treat on many subjects of great importance cannot be denied. On this point, we refer the reader to the just and forcible observations of Dr. Chalmers in the Introductory Essay. If it were a professed body of divinity, the omission of certain topics would be fatal. But the design is to exhibit before the Christian a "Pattern" of that holiness of life in which consists "*the Imitation of Christ.*" Doctrinal discussions would but have extended its size, and impaired its symmetry and usefulness. The duties which the author constantly places before his reader, and we think with the happiest elucidation and persuasiveness, are, self-denial, humility, weanedness from the world, prayer, love, watchfulness, resignation and whatever else is involved in complete conformity to Christ. The great principles on which he openly founds and urges these duties are, man's original innocence, and present depravity; the impotence, hatefulness, and misery of the soul in its fallen state; the necessity of regeneration by the Holy Ghost; and the supreme obligation of believers to him who hath bought them with his blood. So long as pure religion retains a place on earth, must such a book be admired and studied.

Several ancient Latin lives of Kempis have been perused in order to enrich the Memoir. They are extremely unsatisfactory, but have furnished a few additional facts of interest, which have been incorporated.

This edition is now presented to the Christian public in the hope that a work so universally esteemed may, in its amended form, obtain such a circulation as shall give it great and lasting utility.

Howard Malcom, Editor.

INTRODUCTORY ESSAY.

We have sometimes heard the strenuous argumentation of the author of the following Treatise in behalf of holiness excepted against, on the ground that it did not recognize sufficiently the doctrine of justification by faith. There is, in many instances, an over-sensitive alarm on this topic, which makes the writer fearful of recommending virtue, and the private disciple as fearful of embarking on the career of it—a sort of jealousy lest the honors and importance of Christ's righteousness should be invaded, by any importance being given to the personal righteousness of the believer: as if the one could not be maintained as the alone valid plea on which the sinner could lay claim to an inheritance in heaven, and at the same time the other be urged as his indispensable preparation for its exercises and its joys.

It is the partiality with which the mind fastens upon one article of truth, and will scarcely admit the others to so much as a hearing—it is the intentness of its almost exclusive regards on some separate portion of the divine testimony, and its shrinking avoidance of all the distinct and additional portions—it is, in particular, its fondness for the orthodoxy of what relates to a sinner's acceptance, carried to such a degree of favoritism, as to withdraw its attention altogether from what relates to a sinner's sanctification—it is this which, on the pretense of magnifying a most essential doctrine, has, in fact, diffused a mist over the whole field of revelation; and which, like a mist in nature, not only shrouds the general landscape from all observation, but also bedims, while it adds to the apparent size of the few objects that continue visible. It is the same light which reveals the whole, that will render these last more brightly discernible than before; and whether they be the prominences of spiritual truth, or of visible materialism, they are sure to be seen most distinctly in that element of purity and clearness, through the medium of which the spectator is able to recognize even the smaller features and the fainter lineaments that lie on the ground of contemplation.

It is true, that the same darkening process which buries what is remote in utter concealment, will, at least, sully and somewhat distort the nearer perspective, that is before us. But how much more certain is it, that if such be the grossness of the atmosphere as to make impalpable the trees, and the houses, and the hillocks, of our immediate vicinity—then will the distant spires, and mountains, and villages, lie buried in still deeper and more hopeless obscurity. And so it is, with revealed truth, the light of which is spread over a wide and capacious arena, reaching afar from the character of man upon earth to the counsels of God in heaven. When Christ told Nicodemus what change must take place upon the earthly subject, ere it could be prepared for the glories and felicities of the upper sanctuary, he was resisted in this announcement by the incredulity of his auditor. Upon this he came forth with the remonstrance: "If I have told you earthly things, and ye believe not, how shall ye believe, if I tell you of heavenly things?" And then he proceeds to tell of heavenly things—of the transactions that had taken place in the celestial judicatory above, and which behooved to take place ere the sinner could obtain a rightful entrance into the territory of the blessed and the unfallen; of the love that God bare to the world; of the mission thereto on which He delegated His only and well-beloved Son; of the design of this embassy, and the way in which it subserved the great object of recovering sinners from their state of condemnation. These are proceedings which may properly be referred to the seat of the divine government, and to the principles which operate and have ascendency there. The doctrine of regeneration is fulfilled or verified upon the human spirit that is intimately and consciously present with us. The doctrine of the atonement, or the manner in which the reconciliation of the guilty is brought into adjustment with the holiness of God, and with what He requires for maintaining the character and the dignity of his jurisprudence, is fulfilled or verified upon the divine Spirit, whose thoughts and whose ways are inscrutable to man—He not having ascended up into heaven. And the expostulation amounts to this: If a man believe not in the doctrine of regeneration, how can he believe in the doctrine of the atonement? If he consent not to the one, he gives no real credit to the other. He may fancy it, or feign it out to his imagination, but he has no faith in it.

The Bible makes known to us both man's depravity and God's displeasure against him; and if with the eye of our mind we see not the one truth, which lies immediately at hand, neither with the eye of our mind can we see the other truth, which lies in fathomless obscurity, away from us, among the recesses of that mysterious Spirit, who is eternal and unsearchable. But the Bible also makes known to us, both the renewing process by which man's depravity is done away, and the reconciling process by which God's displeasure against him is averted. If we believe not the former, neither do we believe the latter. If to our intellectual view there be a darkness over the terrestrial operation, then is there an equal, or a more aggravated darkness, over that movement which took place in heaven, when the incense of a sweet-smelling savor ascended to the throne, and the wrath of the Lawgiver, who sitteth thereon, was turned away. And what is true of each of these doctrines, regarded abstractly, or in the general, is also true of their personal application. If we find not that a renewing process is taking effect upon us, neither ought we to figure that we have any part in the reconciling process. It is possible to conceive the latter, even while the old nature still domineers over the whole man, and its desires are indulged without remorse, or, at least, without any effective resistance. But this conception is not the faith of the mind. It is rather what the older writers would call a figment of the mind. The Apostle adverts to unfeigned faith. But surely, if a man shall overlook the near, and dwell in thought, on the unseen distance that is beyond it; if, unmindful of any transition in his own breast from sin to sacredness, he nevertheless shall persist in the confidence of a transition from anger to complacency in the mind of the Divinity toward him; if, without looking for a present holiness on earth, he pictures for himself a future beatitude in heaven—he resembles the man who, across the haze of nature's atmosphere, which wraps all things in obscurity, thinks to descry the realities of the ulterior space, when he has only peopled it with gratuitous imagery of his own. The faith of such a one is feigned. He believes not the earthly things which are enunciated in Scripture; and, therefore, though he should take up with the heavenly things that are enunciated there, they are taken up by the wrong faculty. To him they are not the substantial objects of perception, but the illusions of fancy.

The traveler who publishes of distant countries, that we have never seen, may also have included our own familiar neighborhood in his tour, and given a place in his description to its customs, and its people, and its scenery. But if his narrative of the vicinity that is known were full of misrepresentations and errors, we could have no belief in his account of the foreign domains over which he had expatiated. When we believe not what he tells us of our native shire, how can we believe when he tells us of shires or provinces abroad? And by this we may try the soundness of our faith in the divine testimony. It is a testimony which embraces the things of earth and the things of heaven; which teaches us the nature of man as originally corrupt, and requiring a power from above, that may transform it, as well as on the nature of God, as essentially averse to sin, and requiring an atonement that may reconcile and pacify it. If we believe not what is said of the nature of man, and of the doctrine of regeneration that is connected therewith, then we believe not what is said of the nature of God, and of the doctrine of redemption that is connected therewith. We may choose to overlook the former revelation, and stretch our attention onward to the latter, as that with which our fancy is most regaled, or our fears are most effectually quieted into pleasing oblivion. In this way, we may seize on the topic of imputed righteousness, by an effort of desire, or an effort of imagination; but if the man who does so have an unseeing eye toward the topic of his own personal sanctification, he has just as little of faith toward the former article as toward the latter, whatever preference of liking or fancy he may entertain regarding it. It may play around his mind as one of its most agreeable day-dreams, but it has not laid hold of his conviction. The light that maketh the doctrine which affirms the change of God's mind toward the sinner believingly visible, would also make the doctrine which affirms the change of the sinner's mind toward God believingly visible. If the one be veiled from the eye of faith, the other is at least equally so. It may be imaged by the mind, but it is not perceived. It may be conceived, but it is not credited.

There is a well-known publication, called "The Traveler's Guide," which you may take as your companion to some distant land, but the accuracy of which you try upon the earlier stages of your journey. If wholly incorrect in the description which it gives of the first scenes through which you pass, you withdraw all your confidence from its representation of the future scenes and it may even be so wide of the truth, in respect of the things that are present and visible, as should lead you to infer that you are altogether off the road that conducts to the place after which you are aiming. The Bible is a traveler's guide—and it portrays the characters of humility, and self-denial, and virtuous discipline, and aspiring godliness, which mark the outset of the pilgrimage—and it also portrays the characters of brightness, and bliss, and glory, which mark its termination. If you do not believe that it delineates truly the path of transition in time, neither do you believe, however much you may desiderate and dwell upon the prospect, that it sketches truly the place of joyful habitation in eternity. Or, at least, you may well conclude, if you are not now on the path of holiness, that you are not on the path to heaven. And if you believe not the Scripture, when it announces a new spirit as your indispensable preparation here, there may be a dazzling and deceitful imagination, but there is no real belief of what it announces, or of what it promises, about paradise hereafter.

It is thus that we would try the faith of Antinomians. Fancy is not faith. A willful and determined adherence of the mind to some beatific vision, in which it loves to indulge, is not a believing assent of the mind to what a professed Teacher from heaven has revealed to us of the coming immortality. How can we believe, upon his authority, that we are to enter this region of purity and peace, if we believe not, on the same authority, that the road which leads to it, is a road of mortification, and of new obedience, and of strenuous conflict with the desires and urgencies of nature? If the eye of faith, or of the understanding, be opened on some field of truth that is laid before it, it will not overlook the propinquities of this contemplation, while it only admits the objects which lie on the remoter part of the territory. It is evidence which opens this eye; and that evidence which has failed to open it to what is near, will equally fail to open it to what is distant. But though the eye of the understanding be shut, the eye of the imagination may be open. This requires no evidence, and the man who is without faith in the realities which lie on the other side of death, may nevertheless be all awake in his fancy to those images of bliss with which he has embellished it, and may even possess his own heart with the pleasing anticipation of it as his destined inheritance. It is not upon his fancy, however, but upon his faith, that the fulfillment of this anticipation will turn—a faith which, had it been real, would have had respect unto the prescribed road, as well as unto the revealed inheritance—a faith which would have found him in holiness here, as well as in heaven hereafter. That semblance of it which the Antinomian has is a mere vagary, that may amuse or may harden him in the midst of his present worldliness, but which will be dissipated into naught at the judgment seat, when, for the treacherous phantom which deceived him in time, a tremendous reality will be awarded to him for eternity.

We like not that writer to be violently alleged against, who expounds, and expounds truly, the amount of Christian holiness, because he says not enough, it is thought, of the warrants and securities that are provided in the Gospel for Christian hope. We think, that to shed a luminousness over one portion of the divine testimony, is to reflect, at least, if not immediately to shed, a light on all the other portions of it. The doctrine of our acceptance, by faith in the merits and propitiation of Christ, is worthy of many a treatise, and many are the precious treatises upon it which have been offered to the world. But the doctrine of regeneration, by the Spirit of Christ, equally demands the homage of a separate lucubration—which may proceed on the truth of the former, and, by the incidental recognition of it, when it comes naturally in the way of the author's attention, marks the soundness and the settlement of his mind thereupon, more decisively than by the dogmatic, and ostentatious, and often misplaced asseverations of an ultra orthodoxy. And the clearer revelation to the eye of faith of one article, will never darken or diminish, but will, in fact, throw back the light of an augmented evidence on every other article. Like any object that is made up of parte, which we have frequently looked to in their connection, and as making up a whole—the more distinctly one part of it is made manifest, the more forcibly will all the other parts of it be suggested to the mind. And thus it is, that when pressing home the necessity of one's own holiness, as his indispensable preparation for heaven, we do not dissever his mind from the atonement of Christ, but in reality do we fasten it more closely than ever on the necessity of another's righteousness, as his indispensable plea for heaven.

Such we apprehend to be the genuine influence of a Treatise that is now submitted anew to the Christian public. It certainly does not abound in formal and direct avowals of the righteousness which is by faith, and on this account we have heard it excepted against. But we know of no reading that is more powerfully calculated to shut up unto the faith—none more fitted to deepen and to strengthen the basis of a sinner's humility, and so reconcile him to the doctrine of salvation in all its parts, by grace alone—none that, by exhibiting the might and perfection of Christian attainments, can better serve the end of prostrating the inquirer into the veriest depths of self abasement, when, on the humbling comparison of what he is, with what he ought to be, he is touched and penetrated by a sense of his manifold deficiencies. It is on this account that the author of such a work may, instrumentally speaking, do the office of a schoolmaster to bring us unto Christ: nor do we know at what other time it is, than when eyeing from afar the lofty track of spiritual and seraphic piety which is here delineated, that we more feel our need of the great High Priest, or that His peace-making blood and His perfect righteousness are more prized by us.

But it is not enough that we idly gaze on the heavenly course. We must personally enter it; and it is most utterly and experimentally untrue, that, in the prosecution of this walk, we meet with anything to darken the principles on which are made to hinge a sinner's justification in the sight of God. He who looks most frequently to Christ for the purpose of imitation, will also gather most from him on which to prop his confidence, and that too on the right and evangelical basis. There is a sure link of concatenation in the processes of divine grace, by which a growing spiritual discernment is made to emerge out of a growing conformity to the will and the image of the Saviour. These two elements act and react the one upon the other. "He that keepeth my commandments, to him will I manifest myself." "He whose eye is single shall have his whole body full of light."[2] "The Holy Ghost," who acts as a revealer, "is given to those who obey him." "To him who hath, more shall be given" All proving that there is a procedure in the administration of divine grace, by which he who giveth himself up unto all righteousness is guided unto all truth.

And, it is to be hoped, that while the doctrine of justification is not argued, but rather enhanced and recommended by the perusal of such a work, its own distinct object will be still more directly subserved, of leading some to a more strict and separate devotedness of life, than is often to be met with in this professing age. The severities of Christian practice, which are here urged upon the reader, are in no way allied with the penances and the self-inflictions of a monastic ritual, but are the essentials of spiritual discipline in all ages, and must be undergone by every man who is transformed by the Holy Ghost from one of the children of this world to one of the children of light. The utter renunciation of self—the surrender of all vanity—the patient endurance of evils and wrongs—the crucifixion of natural and worldly desires—the absorption of all our interests and passions in the enjoyment of God—and the subordination of all we do, and of all we feel, to his glory—these form the leading virtues of our pilgrimage, and in the very proportion of their rarity, and their painfulness, are they the more effectual tests of our regeneration. And one of the main uses of this book is, that while it enforces these spiritual graces in all their extent, it lays open the spiritual enjoyment that springs from the cultivation of them—revealing the hidden charm which lies in godliness, and demonstrating the sure though secret alliance which obtains between the peace of heaven in the soul, and patience under all the adversities of the path which leads to it. It exposes alike the sufferings and the delights which attach to a life of sacredness: and its wholesome tendency is to reconcile the aspirant after eternal life, to the whole burden of that cross on earth which he must learn to bear

---

2　By singleness of eye here, is meant not a single intentness of the mind upon one truth, but, as is evident from the context, that singleness of aim after an interest in heaven, which is not perverted or seduced from its object by the love of a present evil world.

with submission and cheerfulness, until he exchanges it in heaven for a crown of glory. Such a work may be of service in these days of soft and silken professor-ship—to arouse those who are at ease in Zion; to remind them of the terms of the Christian discipleship, as involving a life of conflict and watchfulness, and much labor; to make them jealous of themselves, and jealous of that evil nature, the power of which must be resisted; but from the besetting presence of which we shall not be conclusively delivered, until death shall rid us of a frame-work, the moral virus of which may be kept in check while we live, but cannot be eradicated by any process short of dissolution.

Thomas Chalmers.

THE LIFE OF THOMAS À KEMPIS.

By Carl Ullmann

Thomas Hamerken (Malleolus[3]) was born in the year 1380, at Kempen or Kamp-en, a small but pleasant town situate in the great plain of the Rhine, not far from Cologne; and for that reason, according to the custom of the times, he is generally called Thomas à *Kempis*. His parents were honest citizens, of limited fortune. Far from being ashamed of his humble origin, it rather disposed him from early youth to modesty. Like Luther, in lowliness of mind, he rejoiced in his humble rank, never aimed at high things, and shunned rather than courted intercourse with the great. His father, a mechanic, earning his daily bread in the sweat of his brow, gave him an example of industry, diligence, simplicity, and perseverance. His mother was distinguished for piety, and planted at an early age in his susceptible heart the seeds of a vital and prevailing love for divine things. Even in tender youth Thomas must have evinced fine talents. It would otherwise scarcely have entered the minds of his parents to make him a scholar; for, as they were very poor, the boy would have to be wholly thrown upon the liberality of others. To young persons in such circumstances, the institutions of the Brethren of the Common Lot[4] at this period offered a helping hand, providing them with the means of subsistence, instruction, and religious training, and offering the prospect of useful occupation and permanent support. Accordingly, at the age of thirteen, Thomas set out for Deventer, where the most celebrated establishment of the kind then flourished. The grammar school of this town, although really an independent institution, was connected in various ways with the Brother-house of the place. The Brethren had the charge of part of the instruction, and zealously contributed to the maintenance and advancement of the scholars, especially the poorer among them. Thomas does not appear at the first to have had any connection with the Brother-house, but after some time he paid a visit to his brother John, then Canon of the monastery of Windesheim, which was in connection with the Society of the Common Lot, and was by him recommended to Florentius, its much revered superintendent. Florentius won the heart of the youth by kindness, as much as he imposed upon him respect by his venerable manners. He furnished him with books which he

---

3   Particulars respecting the life of Thomas are to be found in Daventria illustr. p. 60-62, but especially in the two biographies in Henry Sommalius' edition of his works, the first from the pen of Jodocus Badius Ascensius (1535; see Delprat s. 52, and the passages there cited), the second from that of a later successor of Thomas in the subpriorate of the convent upon Mount St. Agnes, by name Franciscus Tolensis. Compare besides Trithemius de Scriptorib. eccL cap. 707, p. 164. Andreae Bib. belg. p. 836. Foppens Bibl. belg. ii. 1135. Fabricii Bibl. med. iv. 215-219. Schroeckh Kirchengesch. xxxiv. 302. Erhard Gesch. des Wiederaufbluhens i. 263. Schwarz Gesch. der Erziehung 2te Aufl. ii. 244. Delprat uber die Stiftungen Groots an verschiedenen Stellen, s. 13, 34, 84, 103, 126. Beil. Vi. Gieaeler Kirchengesch. ii. 4, s. 347.

4   For a particular account of the Brethren of the Common Lot, see Book III. of Ullmann's "Reformers before the Reformation." Edinburg: T. & T. Clark, 1855.

was too poor to purchase, and procured for him lodgings in the house of a pious matron, just as happened to Luther in Eisenach. There were also other direct, advantages which he derived from his acquaintance with so influential a person, and of which he has himself related the following example. The then Rector of the school at Deventer, John Boehme, who, according to Thomas' account, exercised rigid discipline, was an intimate friend of Florentius. The boy, having one day gone to him to pay his school fees, and redeem the book which he had in the meanwhile placed in pawn, was asked by the Rector, "Who gave you the money?" On hearing that it was Florentius, Boehme dismissed the scholar with the words, "Go, take it back to him: for his sake I shall charge you nothing." Ere long Thomas also took part in the devotional exercises of the Brethren, and was wholly drawn into their pious mode of life, which filled him with admiration. Men such as they were, living in the world and yet appearing to have nothing worldly about them, he had never before seen. Following the bent of his inmost being, and with entire affection, he attached himself to them, and before long entered into full outward communion with the Society. He obtained from Florentius a place in the Brother-house, in which at the time about twenty clerical and three lay members, a procurator, cook, and tailor, dwelt together, and received maintenance. His chief companion, and soon his most intimate friend, was Arnold of Schoonhoven (Schoenhofen), a youth of fervent piety, with whom he shared a little chamber and bed. Here Thomas exercised himself in copying and reading the Holy Scriptures, and unremittingly took part in the devotional exercises of the Brethren. What he earned by writing he put into the common fund, and when it fell below what was needful for his support, the lack was supplied by the generosity of Florentius. The example of his young friend Arnold's glowing piety, especially made a deep impression upon his mind. Arnold used to rise every morning at four, the moment the clock struck the hour, and after uttering a short prayer upon his knees by his bedside, quickly dressed himself and hastened to the worship. At all devotional exercises he was the first to come and the last to depart. Besides, he frequently withdrew to some solitary place in order to devote himself unobserved to prayer and meditation. Thomas sometimes accidentally became the witness of these outpourings of his friend's heart, and says, "I found myself on such occasions kindled by his zeal to prayer, and wished to experience, were it but sometimes, a grace of devotion like that which he seemed almost daily to possess. Nor was his fervor in prayer at all wonderful, considering that wheresoever he went or staid, he was most diligent in keeping his heart and mouth." One of the things which Arnold of Schoenhofen desired, was to learn quickly and well the art of writing, which was so highly valued and so usefully applied by the Brethren. He disclosed this wish to his friend, who thought within himself, "Ah, willingly would I also learn to write, did I but first know how to make myself better!" "But," as Thomas observes respecting his companion, "he obtained a special grace from God which made him skillful in every good work, so that he never felt it hard to obey." It is evident from these disclosures that Thomas, in his own estimation, fell far short of his friend, and that, in comparison with him, he was not satisfied with his zeal in devotion. This is likewise evinced by a dream which he is reported to have had about this time. The Virgin Mary appeared to him, and while she lavished caresses upon the scholars around, looked sternly and severely at him for being remiss in his devotion and prayers to her.[5]

While Arnold of Schoenhofen afforded Thomas a youthful pattern of piety, studious zeal, and that exact obedience which the Brethren so urgently inculcated, side by side with it he had a still higher and more finished model in Father Florentius himself. The apostolical simple-mindedness and dignity, the urbanity, gentleness, and self-sacrificing activity for the common weal which characterized this person, inspired Thomas with a boundless admiration. Of this in his life of Florentius, itself the noblest monument of affectionate reverence for the departed, he relates many characteristic and affecting traits. Before he had as yet become a boarder with the Brethren, his teacher John Boehme, who was always a rigid disciplinarian, and exercised a strict government over the boys, even in the church, had ordered him with some others to attend in the choir. Here Florentius also was present. "Now, whenever," as Thomas proceeds to relate, "I saw my good master Florentius standing in the choir, even although he did not look about, I was so awed in his presence by his venerable aspect that I never dared to speak a word. On one occasion I stood close beside him, and he turned to me and sang from the same book. He even put his hand upon my shoulder, and then I stood as if rooted to the spot, afraid even to stir, so amazed was I at the honor done me." Thomas, in the course of time, came to dwell in Florentine house, and closer acquaintance did not diminish his reverence, but strengthened his love. When he happened to be troubled in his mind, he applied, like the other youths on similar occasions, to his respected master, and such was the effect of even a sight of his placid and cheerful countenance, or at least of a few words of conversation, that he never failed to leave his presence comforted and encouraged. The attachment of the youth toward his spiritual father extended to the minutest points. In consequence of weakly health, Florentius sometimes could not partake of the common meals. On such occasions, he ate at a small and cleanly covered table in the kitchen, and Thomas considered it an honor to attend and serve him. "Unworthy though I was," he says, "I often, at his invitation, prepared the table, brought from the dining room what little he required, and served him with cheerfulness and joy." If Florentius was at any time worse than usual, it was customary to call upon the brethren in the neighboring houses to remember him in prayer. On these occasions, Thomas often undertook to carry the message, and delighted to be so employed. His veneration for Florentius, however, was principally evinced by the pains he took deeply to engrave on his mind the sayings and conduct of his master, imbibe the entire image of his life, and express the spirit of it in his own actions and thoughts no less than in his writings.

Thomas says that examples are more instructive than words. This was the case with himself. He had a boding mind, and was animated by that piety which always presumes the best of others, fondly looks up to some higher character, and endeavors to raise itself by imitation to the same level. Such was the effect produced upon him by the Brethren's whole manner of life, which appeared to him in the fairest light, by Arnold of Schoenhofen, and particularly by Florentius. Even little incidents that occurred made an impression of the same kind. In his biography of Henry Brune, he relates as follows. "One day, in winter, Henry was sitting by the fireside, warming his hands, but with his face turned toward the wall, for he was at the time engaged in secret prayer. When I saw this, I was greatly edified,

---

5   The narrative is to be found in the Speculum Exemplorum Dist. x. § 7, and is inserted between the two Biographies in the Sommal. Edition.

and from that day loved him all the more." The picture in the fancy of the youth may in such cases have arisen above its object. But it had a quickening and improving effect upon himself, and that was of most importance.

Florentius, who on his part no less treated Thomas like a beloved son, appears also to have mainly determined his outward course of life. The youth had now passed seven years in the zealous exercise of piety and the prosecution of his studies at the school and Brother-house of Deventer, which had been to him an actual paradise, when one day, being a high festival, Florentius, noticing in him a more than ordinary liveliness in the worship, called him at the close of the service, and addressed him somewhat as follows: "My most beloved son, Thomas, the period has now arrived when you must decide upon a vocation in life. You are standing at the Pythagorean point where the two roads separate. You see what distresses and dangers abound in the world; and how even its joys are transitory, and accompanied with repentance. You know we must all die, and render an account of our life to God and Christ. Woe to them who cannot do it with a good conscience! What will it profit a man to gain the whole world and lose his own soul? Be anxious then about your salvation. There is, however, as you have often heard, a twofold way of attaining to it, the active and the contemplative. The one is trodden by those who, by good works, make themselves worthy of Christ; the other, and the more acceptable to God, by those who, with Mary, set themselves at the feet of Jesus. Whichsoever of the two you may prefer, you will walk it better and more safely in the convent than in the world which lieth in wickedness. Do not believe that the inmates of the cloister are idlers. In their prayers, devotional exercises, and manual labors, they have an excellent occupation, and may earn the reward of the active life. And as little believe that you have nothing to offer to God. You have yourself, your body, your will. Present these to Him, and you will reap in return eternal life. I know, too, that you are not insensible to what your Creator and Saviour has done for you, for I have often observed in you symptoms of true piety. If, then, you ask of me what religious Order 1 would recommend, I am of opinion that, for persons who have been educated in our schools, the most eligible is that instituted by our venerable Father, Gerhard Groot—I mean that of the Canons according to the rule of St. Augustine, for which, as you are aware, we have lately erected two colleges." This address of the much revered master decided the mind of the youth. He answered, stammering with emotion; "Father, you open to me the prospect of what I have long desired. I have a brother in Windesheim. Please, therefore, be so good as to procure for me a place among my dear schoolfellows upon Mount St. Agnes." Next day Florentius gave Thomas a letter of recommendation to the Prior of this convent.

The convent of St. Agnes stood in a pleasant and healthy situation, at no great distance from the town of Zwoll,[6] and upon an upland, the foot of which was watered by the Vechte, a stream abounding in fish. Recently erected, with very slender means, it was as yet but little known and esteemed. This, however, was far from discouraging Thomas; for he was very kindly received, and the place had all the attractions of a refuge prepared for him by God. From that day he passed in it the whole of his life, and by his means the obscure monastery has acquired a reputation in history.

Strongly as the mind of Thomas was bent upon his vocation, and although

---

6   A fortified town of the Netherlands, capital of the province of Over--Yssel, fifty-two miles north-east from Amsterdam. In 1855 its population was about seventeen thousand. It was formerly a free imperial city, and belonged to the Hanseatic League.

both nature and previous education had perfectly adapted him for it, he did not plunge into it without consideration. Deliberate even in his youthful zeal, he spent five years of a novitiate, assumed the monastic dress in the sixth, and did not until the year following take the vow, which he then, however, kept with inviolable fidelity. As he was now a priest, besides the common and special devotional exercises, his chief occupation in the monastery consisted in delivering religious discourses and the duties of the confessional. He also, however, employed himself in the composition of works and treatises, and in transcribing those of others. Like a worthy disciple of the Brotherhood, he practiced the copying of books with the utmost care and diligence, and had here the advantage of a quick eye and skillful hand. He took a child-like delight in well-written books, and was of opinion that what is good and holy ought to be ornamented and honored in this manner. The monastery of St. Agnes preserved an admirable transcript of the Bible in four volumes, executed by him, a great Mass-book, and several works of St. Bernard. He also repeatedly transcribed his own work on the "Imitation of Jesus Christ." Nor did Thomas even withdraw himself from the direction of the affairs of the monastery; for he was a great economist of time, and, to the neglect of his health, busied himself from the earliest hour in the morning. He first held the office of sub-prior,[7] and before he was far advanced in life that of procurator or steward. But as the outward duties connected with the employment appeared to abstract him too much from meditation and his more profitable labors as an author, he was reponed in the sub-priorate, and held the situation until his decease.

From the nature of the case, we have little to say of Thomas's cloisteral life. Without any considerable disturbance, it flowed on like a limpid brook, reflecting on its calm surface the unclouded heavens. Quiet industry, lonely contemplation, and secret prayer, filled up the day, and every day was like another. Of the instances with which he was accustomed to enliven his discourses, many seem to have been borrowed from his own experience; but, as he always speaks in the third person, these are hardly distinguishable from the rest, and furnish little that is characteristic. I shall adduce but two particulars, of which the first is as follows: A pious brother of the house had to officiate at mass. Before performing the duty, he visited another who lay dangerously ill, and was entreated by him to offer in the service a prayer for his recovery. The brother complied with the request. At the conclusion of mass, the patient felt himself relieved, and in a few days was restored to health; and so strong an impression did the circumstance make upon his mind, that from that time he became more and more zealous in his devotions and pious studies, and after some years rose to the dignity of prior. In this instance, Thomas may have been either the one or the other of the two parties. The second incident has, from the earliest times, been supposed to have occurred to Thomas himself: One of the brethren had lost in his cell a book upon which he placed a particular value. After having long sought for it in vain, he at last addressed himself by prayer to the Virgin Mary, and several times repeated the Salutation of the angel; whereupon, while sitting upon his bed opposite the Virgin's picture it seemed to enter his mind, like an inspiration, Search below the straw of the bed! He obeyed, found the lost treasure, and was thereby greatly encouraged in the worship of Mary. Both narratives present to us a peculiar feature in the piety

---

7   Only one of the priors of the monastery during Thomas' connection with it, being the third since its institution, is mentioned by him. He was called Theodoricus Clivis, and is designated as devotus et praedilectus Pater noster. Sermon, ad Novit. iii. 3, Ex. 6.

of Thomas, connected with the state of education at the time, and of which many instances might be adduced. We allude to credulity for the marvelous, and, what is partly connected with it, zeal for the worship of the saints. In both respects, but particularly in the adoration of Mary and St. Agnes, the pious brother goes great lengths, and occasionally falls into the playful. Even here, however, all he says has ever an amiable, ingenuous, and thoroughly moral character, and he is far from allowing these things to displace the essentials of true piety.

Thomas, by moderating the rigor of mortification, and by a well-regulated activity, reached a very advanced stage of life. He died in July 1471, at the age of from 91 to 92.[8] Respecting the last years of his life tradition had preserved no particular account.[9]

In his work upon Spiritual exercises, Thomas exhorts the monk "to show forth in his whole walk, modesty and pious cheerfulness," and in another passage depicts the man of God as "of a cheerful countenance, calm and pleasant in his discourse, prudent and regular in all his actions, and ever shedding around him peace and blessing." It seems as if by these traits he had depicted himself. All who were acquainted with him have borne witness how, during the whole course of his life, he evinced love to God and love to man, cheerfully bearing all afflictions, and kindly excusing the faults and foibles of his brethren. In his whole nature and habits,[10] he was cleanly, moderate, chaste, inwardly happy, and outwardly cheerful. His utmost endeavor was to maintain a uniform tranquillity and complete peace of mind. With this view, he did not willingly entangle himself with the business of the world, avoided intercourse with the great and honorable, observed a marked silence when the conversation turned on temporal things, and was ever fond of solitude and meditation. At the same time, he was anything but stupid. From early youth he had a very lively sense of friendship, for which, it is true, he found no solid or lasting basis except in a mutual love of divine things. He was full of zeal and activity in promoting the welfare of his community, and especially in whatever tended to enliven or adorn the divine worship; and in his own favorite province, when God and divine things were the subject of conversation, he was an eloquent and inexhaustible speaker. Multitudes from remote places flocked to hear him. And whenever he was solicited, he was always ready to deliver a discourse, only taking a short time for meditation or sleep. He also gave regular addresses with great care and faithfulness. We still possess a series of *Sermones* and *Collatio-*

---

8   Such must have been his age, if, according to the dates assigned by all, his death took place about the end of July (octavo Calendas Augusti) 1471, and he was born in 1380. This is also the opinion of the early writers, one of whom, Jodocus Badius, xii. 5, calls him a man of ninety, and the other, Franciscus Tolensis, § 8, a man of ninety-two. Of this period he passed no less than seventy-one years on Mount St. Agnes, six of a novitiate, and sixty-five as an actual Canon. Previous to which he had lived seven years in the house of Florentius. According to this computation he could not have been, as Jodocus Badius supposes, twelve, but thirteen or fourteen years of age on his arrival at Deventer, unless we suppose, what is less probable, that ho spent two years there before his admission into, the Brother-house. Accordingly, the dates in the life of Thomas may, with the greatest likelihood, be stated as follows: He arrived in his thirteenth year at Deventer, and was in the year following admitted into the house of Florentius. Here he remained seven years, and then, when between twenty and twenty-one, went to Mount St. Agnes, where he lived six years as a novice, and sixty-five as a Canon, consequently the whole period betwixt 26th and 91st, or 27th and 92nd year.

9   Respecting the exhumation of his bones, which took place about the year 1672, and their reinterment at Zwoll, see Foppens Bibl. belg, ii 1138.

10   These traits are borrowed in part from his own writings, but mainly from Francisci Tolensis Vita Thom. § 9, sqq.

nes from his hand, for the special use of novices, which, in clear and flowing diction, and with rich applications to life, impressively propound the doctrine of his practical and devotional mysticism.

In devout exercises, public and private, Thomas was unwearied. Like the friend of his youth, Arnold of Schoenhofen, he was all his life the earliest at the commencement, and the last at the close, of divine service. During the singing of the Psalms,[11] he stood in an erect posture, never studying his ease by leaning or supporting his body; his look was often raised heavenward; his countenance, in a manner, shone, and his whole frame involuntarily followed the direction of his soul. To a person who, making use of a pun current among the monks, observed to him that he seemed as fond of the Psalms as if they were salmon, he replied, "It is a fact, but my disgust is also excited, when I see men not duly attentive to them." It must be mentioned as part of his private discipline, that on certain days of the week, while singing the hymn *Stetit Jesus*, he used the scourge.

Thomas' outward appearance corresponded to the gentleness of his inward nature. He was below the middle size, but well-proportioned. The color of his face was fresh, with a slight tinge of brown. His eyes were piercingly bright, and, in spite of incessant use, retained their acuteness of vision to extreme old age, so that he never used spectacles. Franciscus Tolensis was once shown a picture[12] of him even then much effaced, but with the characteristic motto at the foot, "I have sought rest everywhere and found it nowhere, save in solitude and books."

These things taken conjunctly exhibit a man who undoubtedly cultivated and displayed only one aspect of human nature and life. That aspect, however, has also its rights, and was displayed by Thomas in a way which entitles him to be considered its perfect type and finished model. The unity of his character was the more complete that, as a whole, it was undisturbed, inasmuch as, from early youth, he had pursued essentially the same course. Thomas paid no attention to the world. He valued science only in as far as it subserved religious purposes. He was no scholar in the proper sense of the term, and did not even aspire to be an orator. All he did and endeavored had, as its single and exclusive drift, to cherish the one thing needful in his own heart, and to train others in apostolical simplicity for the same object. Compared with this, he disregarded all other things. The love of God, and reared on that foundation, peace of mind, and the calm happiness of unbroken fellowship with Him, was the ultimate and exclusive object of all his efforts. And this object he attained as few else have done. His own being was wholly imbued with the love of God and Christ, and pervaded by calmness and peace; and of this love and peace he has been not only the most impressive preacher, but, I might say, the attractive magnet to countless multitudes. This leads us to his writings and their contents.

If called upon to state the thoughts, principles, and maxims, upon which the life of Thomas was based, the question is not so much of a system of doctrine,

---

11   Thomas repeatedly expresses his strong taste for sacred music; and does so in a peculiarly characteristic manner in the Sermon, ad Novit., P 1. Serm. 6. Exempl. 3, where probably he is himself one of the parties.

12   His likeness, together with a prospect of the monastery of St. Agnes, was engraved on a plate of copper that lies over his body. In this engraving is represented a person respectfully presenting to him a label on which is written a verse to this effect: "O where is peace, for thou its paths hast trod?" To which Thomas returns another label, inscribed as follows: "Jn poverty, retirement, and with God."—*Malcom's Memoir.*

properly so called, as of a theory of religion and morality. It is true that with him, in common with all eminent men, a few governing thoughts constitute the kernel of his intellectual being, and that, impelled by the ardor of his love, he never tires of propounding and enforcing them in ever-fresh, although but slightly varied, forms. But then his thoughts do not appear as abstract notions, far less as a complete body of these, but are presented as maxims, in a gush of devotional oratory, sometimes bordering on the poetical. In a word, what we find in him is practical wisdom in proverbs, which, however, is sustained by a determinate general tendency of life and Spirit. In this mental tendency, if analyzed into its constituent parts, and duly estimated, we must distinguish two elements: the one essential, universal, and of enduring importance, the other more formal, pertaining to the particular age, and of transitory nature; the one is Christianity, the other Monachism. It is true that, even in Thomas' case, these elements are not separate and disjoined, but throughout fused into each other by the common medium of practical Mysticism. Christianity with him is imbued with Monachism, although more so in some points and less in others, and, as must be allowed, is thereby troubled and narrowed, but Monachism is always animated and refined by Christianity. Still, sometimes the one, and sometimes the other, preponderates, and it is possible, without violently dissevering, to contemplate them apart.

The *works of Thomas*,[13] which show, not indeed the absence of general Christianity, but yet the predominance of Monachism, are his sermons to novices, and his discourses to conventual brethren in general, his "*Disciplina Claustralium*," and "*Dialogus Novitiorum*," together with several smaller pieces, particularly letters and poems. In this class we must also reckon the biographies of the most eminent of the Brethren of the Common Lot, in which he exhibits the ideals of the ascetic life.[14] The works in which, on the contrary, monasticism is not wanting, but where general Christian mysticism forms the principal ingredient, are, the "Imitation of Jesus Christ,"[15] the "Soliloquy of the Soul," the "Garden of Roses," the "Valley of Lilies," the tract "*De Tribus Tabernaculis*" and some minor treatises. Among these the book on the "Imitation of Jesus Christ,"[16] standing— as no one doubts, and as even its effects have demonstrated it to do—in point of excellence far above all the rest, is the purest and most finished production of Thomas, and next to it, although in much lower degree, we would place the "Garden of Roses," which is even more sententious and apothegmatic in its style.

---

13   I here use the edition of Thomas' Opera omnia by the Jesuit Sommalius, Cologne, 1728, 4.

14   Thomas has written at large biographies of Gerhard and Florentius, and more briefly those of Florentius' eminent disciples, John Gronde, John Binkerink, Lubert Berner, Henry Brune, Gerhard Zerbolt, Aemilius Van Buren, Jacob Von Viana, Arnold Schoonhoven, and John Cacabus, the pious cook in the house of Florentius. These biographies are in Sommalius' edition of 1560, in the 3d part, s. 3-142; and in that of 1728 in the last part, s. 1-113, and are succeeded by the life of the saint Lidwina or Lidwigis. In Florentius and his disciples Thomas portrays men whom he intimately knew; and hence his representations, although imperfect in respect of language (he says himself that he describes them barbarizando), are in a high degree natural and vivid, and owing to his love for the subjects, have a childlike affectionateness. We fancy we are beholding pictures from the Dutch school of that age. The abundance of individual traits makes the life of Florentius the most attractive of them all. The reader will have observed how largely we have hitherto drawn our materials from these sources. They are the most important fund of knowledge respecting the inward life of the community of the Brethren.

15   I entertain no doubt that this work proceeds from Thomas, and no one else.

16   This work has seen near forty editions in the original Latin, and above sixty translations have been made from it into modem languages.

In the first-mentioned writings, and consistent with their predominant monastic stand-point, the doctrine of works and their meritoriousness occupies a most important place. In those last mentioned, especially the "Imitation of Christ," that doctrine almost wholly disappears, and, excepting in a few allusions, all is traced back to Divine grace. We may conclude from this, what is proved by their higher excellence in other respects, that these productions belong to the later period of Thomas' life.[17]

Thomas' whole theory cannot in respect of the thoughts be properly called original. Mystical theology is based essentially upon experience, principally the mystic's own, but likewise also that of others. In the latter respect it depends upon tradition. Through the whole of the mediaeval period there runs a traditional mysticism, molding the same material of thought into a variety of forms. In this general current, after it had assumed the particular form given to it, first by Ruysbroek, and subsequently by the founders of the Brotherhood of the Common Lot, Thomas à Kempis occupies a place. He draws continually from the great traditionary stream. Along with his own experiences, he everywhere takes advantage of the insight, the sayings, and the exemplary lives of the Fathers and the Brethren, both far and near, and blends them with his acute observation of life and profound knowledge of the human heart into a far richer whole than any from the same circle had ever hitherto done. But even although this material he not to any great extent original, it yet acquires, through the individuality of Thomas, compacting it into a beautiful unity, a new soul, something peculiarly lovely, amiable, and fresh, a tone of truth, a cheerfulness, and gentle warmth of heart, by virtue of which it produces quite a peculiar effect. This, in our opinion, is the chief quality, especially of the book of the "Imitation of Jesus Christ." It charms us by truth which is the genuine reflex of the author's life, and is self-evidenced in every word, by the heart that beats in it, by the pure, unmingled tone, the silver accent of inward genuineness, the simple child-like spirit which pervades the whole.

This unmixed simplicity of character was, in the case of Thomas, chiefly dependent upon his complete and entire abstraction from many things which create discord in the minds of other men. The world did not bewilder him; art and nature with their glories and charms tempted him not away from his inward musings; science suggested to him no riddles and doubts, occasioned him no conflicts and pains. He kept aloof from them. As the bent of his mind was exclusively heavenward, his relation to civil and political life was purely negative. In his eyes it belonged to the world. His bearing toward it was that of a pilgrim and stranger. In all his writings we do not discover one trace of interest in it. At the most we can only reckon as such the frequently recurring warning that the devotee should beware of courting intercourse with the great and mighty,[18] a warning which he himself conscientiously that followed. Art, especially in so far as it was consecrated to the service of religion, was more likely to have attracted his susceptible mind, especially considering that in the Netherlands it had already displayed great life and riches. The more considerable cities possessed numerous workshops of

---

17   "He composed his treatise on the 'Imitation of Christ', in the sixty-first year of his age, as appears from a note of his own writing in the library of his convent."—*Malcom's Memoir.*

18   *E. g.* Sermon. Ad Novit. Ii. 3, p. 12, and elsewhere. Of the fact, that by his simple book on the "Imitation of Christ," he would one day find his way into the society of the great, Thomas himself had not the fainest foreboding.

painters and statuaries.[19] The brothers Hubert and John van Eyck had executed the miracles of their pencil. Hemmling was Thomas' cotemporary. The glories of Gothic architecture were presented to his eye, but they had no charms for him. At the most he had a taste for psalmody, in which he even tried his hand,[20] only however for sacred music in the ascetic spirit. Even nature appears to have been strange to him. While Euysbroek was fond of musing in the forests of Grunthal, Thomas confined himself wholly to his cell, and warns the reader against even taking a walk, as calculated to disturb and distract the mind, and from winch a man rarely returns improved. Considering the school through which he passed, one might confidently have expected in Thomas an inclination for science, and of this he certainly is not wholly destitute. The ascetical impressions, however, which he had received at Daventer had speedily overgrown those of a scientific character, and he appreciated science only in its moral and practical aspects. Let us observe more narrowly what his relation to it was.

Thomas, according to the standard of the age, was not unlearned. He had very diligently read the Bible, and likewise its patristic and mystical expositors, and recommended to others in the most urgent manner the study of both. He expressed himself in the language of scholars, although not with elegance or purity, as he modestly acknowledges, still with ease and fluency. He loved good and useful books, and took a lively interest in their collection, preservation, and use, considering it as a necessary ornament of a good monastery to possess as rich and beautiful a library as possible, and reckoning it one of the standing duties of a true monk, to read and write books. He likewise encouraged susceptible youths to the zealous prosecution of their studies, and even to the acquisition of a classical education. Several of the most meritorious restorers of ancient literature went forth from his quiet cell, and he lived to see in his old age his scholars, Rudolph Lange, Moritz, Count of Spiegelberg, Louis Dringenberg, Antony Liber, and, above all, Rudolph Agricola and Alexander Hegius, laboring with success for the revival of the sciences in Germany and the Netherlands. Accordingly Thomas was not without scientific culture himself, or the power of inspiring a taste for it in others. He even says, "Science, and just as little the simple knowledge of objects, whatever they may be, so far from being blameable, when considered in itself, is good and ordained of God;" and in another passage, "Nor must we blame that pious and modest investigation of truth which is always ready to receive instruction, and seeks to walk in the sound maxims of the Fathers." His entire position is, however, far from scientific, in the proper sense of the word, and is and remains, even in reference to science, ascetical. He imposes upon it very narrow limits—calls upon it to abstain from the metaphysical, the transcendental, and all deeper research into God and the world, not to occupy itself with the Empyrean

---

19   So early as 1396, Antwerp possessed five painter and sculptor establishments, from which we may infer the number generally in the Netherlands. See Waagen on Hubert and John Van Eyck, Breslau, 1822, s. 62, a work affording much general information respecting the state of art at the time in the Netherlands.

20   We possess a small "*Poetical Remains*" from the pen of Thomas, consisting partly of short poems, some of them *versus memoriales,* containing ascetical and monastic rules, and partly connected with his main theme, viz., the doctrine of the Imitation of Jesus Christ, and partly having more the character of ecclesiastical hymns, *Cantica Spiritualia,* which celebrate the Trinity, the Passion of Christ, John the Baptist and the Evangelist, the Virgin Mary, St. Agnes, and other saints. The pious, childlike, and amiable mind of Thomas is expressed in these poems, but they do not manifest any particular talent or perfection in sacred poetry. In some passages they become puerile and sportive.

heavens and the higher orders of Spiritual beings (which speculative mysticism, and even Ruysbroek, brought within the range of contemplation), and to cherish the desire to know God, not as he is in himself, which the Schoolmen and even the philosophizing ecclesiastical Fathers aspired to do, but simply as he is in us. More especially, he considers science not as a relatively independent element of life, and possessing value on its own account, but appreciates and measures it on all occasions only by the standard of edification, and proportionately underrates the theoretical to the practical. It is not merely that he insists, above all things, on simple faith, inasmuch as "Human reason is weak and liable to err, which true faith is not." It is not merely that he lays down the principle, as we find Anselm also doing, that "all reason and natural investigation ought to follow faith, not to precede or impair it." But he puts no value upon any knowledge that is not of direct moral utility, and if ever he concedes anything to science, always immediately annexes an antithesis by which the concession is as good as done away. If he has pronounced it to be good, he does not fail to say, "But a pure conscience and a virtuous life are always to he preferred." If he has insisted on toleration for it, he proceeds, "But blessed the simplicity which leaves the path of knotty questions and walks safely in the way of the divine commandments! …You are required to have faith and an untainted life, not high intelligence or deep insight into the mysteries of God. If you do not know or comprehend things beneath you, how will you understand those which are above? Submit yourself to God, humble your mind to believe, and the light of knowledge will be given you, in as far as it is salutary and needful." If he has admitted that "Every man has by nature a desire of knowledge," he adds the restriction, "But of what avail is knowledge without the fear of God? Better the simple peasant who serves God than the proud philosopher who, neglecting himself, contemplates the courses of the stars," or "I would rather experience compunction than know how to define it," and "What will it profit you to hold deep disquisitions about the Trinity, if you want that humbleness of mind which alone is pleasing to it?" All which propositions[21] are perfectly true and morally weighty, but at the same time depreciatory of science, inasmuch as they put it into connection with something bad, such as pride or want of self-acquaintance, and oppose to it morality and piety, as if these could not be united with it nor serve as its basis.

But while thus unduly depreciating mere knowledge as a thing insufficient of itself, only ministering to presumption, and inflating the mind, he, on the other hand, enjoins something of a far better sort, and which is at once practical in its nature and comprehensive of perfect humility, viz., Wisdom. Knowledge of itself is profane and humanly restricted. It derives its origin from the world, and entangles us with it. Wisdom, on the contrary, is heavenly and pure. It comes from God, and leads back to him again. In respect of its nature it is moral and holy, for not merely is it a higher and divinely-bestowed intelligence of the one thing needful for man to know, but it is, at the same time, divine freedom and divine peace, including within it the chief good, for which every man, by virtue of the deepest and inmost want of his nature, cannot but long.

Every man aspires after that which is good, and endeavors to exhibit something of the kind in his life. Every man wishes inward contentment and happiness,

---

21   To this belongs also what Thomas says in the *Doctrinale Juven.* ii. 1, "It is a great fault to speak bad Latin in schools, but it is a still greater daily to offend God by sinning, and to feel no sorrow for doing so."

and pants for freedom as the best blessing which could fall to his lot. But the question is, where is all this to be found? And on that point, before every other, we must be informed, in order not to be deceived with the semblance of good, as so many are. It is certain—and this proposition of the Bible Thomas incessantly repeats—that the truth should and will make us free. But where is the proper, essential, imperishable, and ever satisfying truth?

All this, truth, freedom, peace, blessedness, the substantial and imperishable good must be sought—as is in the first place Thomas' opinion—not in the things of the world. Their nature is vain, their possession transient, their enjoyment accompanied with sorrow, their pleasures outweighed by their pains. For life is full of tribulations, and inscribed on every side with the cross. It is like a great cross, which a man is able to bear only when he is himself borne upon another. In the world, and its life of sense, man finds no true satisfaction, but disturbance and distraction, misery and death, and for a recompense, the eternal pains of hell. And just as little ought he to seek his peace among the creatures—that is, his fellow-men. They are frail, changeable, uncertain, and deceptive. Every man is a liar, a sinner, an imperfect being. With such a being the chief good can never be found; as it cannot with any of the creatures at all. For the same reason, neither ought a man to seek it in himself, for he must recognize himself as in all things a dependent and transitory being, and, above all, as corrupt, and in every circumstance of his life sinful, erring, and defective, drawn down by his sensuality, or pushed aloft by his pride, but always governed by caprice and selfishness.

Well might man be lord of the earth, if his senses were but subjected to his reason, and his reason to the will of God. This he was destined to be; but this he is not. "His nature, originally good, was depraved by the first man, and infected with sin, so that, when left to itself, it inclines him to that which is base and wicked. For the little power that remains is but as a spark buried in ashes. That spark is the natural reason, which, surrounded with thick darkness, and though still preserving a sense of the difference between good and evil, truth and falsehood, is yet incompetent to execute all that it approves, and attain to the full light of truth, or to soundness of affection. ... Hence, it is, that with my flesh I serve the law of sin, being more obedient to my senses than to my reason. 'To will is present with me, but how to perform that which is good, I find not.' This is the cause why I often purpose many good things; but through lack of grace to aid my weakness, shrink from the smallest resistance, and lose heart. Hence, I know the way of perfection, and see with sufficient clearness how I ought to act; but oppressed with the weight of my corruption, I fail to rise to that which is the more perfect." Accordingly, that which, in opposition to grace, Thomas styles the nature of man, has in the delineation he makes of it, the following properties. It seeks its own profit and advantage; and is fond of being honored and respected. It looks to the things that are temporal, rejoices in earthly gains, mourns over earthly losses, and is provoked by the slightest injury. It is more willing to receive than to give, and loves its own peculiar things. It courts enjoyment and idleness, and is charmed with the beautiful and curious. It is strongly inclined to the creatures and the flesh, willingly seeks consolation from outward sources, rejoices in the multitude of friends and relatives, in nobility of birth and powerful connections; while, on the contrary, it flies from all that is humble and obscure, from every slight and humiliation, will not consent to be outdone, to obey, to suffer, or to die. In a word, it refers all to self, and strives and contends only for its own profit, and transitory enjoyments.

If, then, such be the case with the world, with men, and with one's own natu-

ral self, where can man find that which is truly good, and which enduringly satis-
fies? Not in the multitude of things, which distract, hut in the one which collects
and unites. For the one does not proceed out of the many, hut the many out of the
one. That one is the thing needful, the chief good, and nothing better and higher
either exists, or can even he conceived. "For such a Being," says Thomas, "my
soul most vehemently longs—for One who is greater, better, and worthier, than
any other can he, and who abounds with all good things." Such a Being is God. He
alone it is who can quiet the longings of the heart, and make it wholly tranquil and
happy. Compared with Him the creature is nothing, and only becomes anything
when in fellowship with Him. "Whatever is not God," says Thomas, "is nothing,
and should be counted as nothing. That man will long remain little and groveling
himself who esteems anything great, save the one infinite and eternal good. … All
that does not proceed from God must perish." Here we find Thomas agreeing in
words with Eckart of the Free Spirit. Both say, God is all and man nothing. But
with what difference of meaning! Eckart understands the proposition metaphys-
ically, and thinks of God as the only Being, the universal substance, in respect
of which all created existence is but accidental; whereas Thomas understands
the proposition morally, and thinks of God as the chief good, who has permitted
rational creatures to have a real subsistence, although not one independent of
Him. According to Eckart, man only requires to bear in mind his true and eternal
nature, in order to be himself God; according to Thomas, God, as himself the most
perfect person, in the exercise of free grace, and from the fullness of the blessings
that reside in Him, is pleased to impart personality to men in order that, although
morally considered, they are themselves nothing, they may, through Him, and in
voluntary fellowship with Him, attain to true existence and eternal life.

To enter into fellowship with God, the chief good and fountain of blessedness, and to become one with Him, is the basis of all true contentment. But how
can two such parties, God and man, the Creator and the creature, be brought together? God is in heaven and man on earth; God is perfect and man sensual, vain,
and sinful. There must, therefore, be mediation, some way in which God comes
to man and man to God, and both unite. This union of man with God depends
upon a twofold condition, one negative and the other positive. The negative is
that man shall wholly renounce what can give him no true peace. He must forsake
the world, which offers to him so much hardship and distress, and whose very
pleasures turn into pains; he must detach himself from the creatures, for nothing
defiles and entangles the heart so much as impure love of them, and only when
a man has advanced so far as no longer to seek consolation from any creature,
does he enjoy God, and find consolation in Him; he must, in fine, die to, and deny
himself, and wholly renounce selfishness and self-love, for whoever loves himself
will find, wherever he seeks, only his own little, mean, and sinful self, without
being able to find God. This last is the hardest of all tasks, and can only be attained
by deep and earnest self-acquaintance. But whosoever strictly exercises self- ex-
amination, will infallibly come to recognize himself in his meanness, littleness,
and nonentity, and will be led to the most perfect humility, entire contrition, and
ardent longing after God. For only when man has become little and nothing in his
own eyes, can God become great to him, only when he has emptied himself of all
created things can God replenish him with His grace. A great many of Thomas'
sayings pertained to this subject. Of these we shall adduce a few. "The further
man recedes from the consolations of earth, the nearer he draws to God; and the
deeper he descends into himself, and the more vile he becomes in his own sight,

the higher does he rise toward God. Wert thou sensible of thine own nothingness, and emptied of all love to the creatures, I would then shed forth my grace largely upon thee. As long as you fix your eyes upon the creatures, you lose the view of the Creator, ... All consists in bearing the cross, and in dying upon it. And there is no other way to life and true peace of mind, but that of the holy cross, and of daily mortification. ... If you dispose yourself for that to which you are appointed, viz., suffering and mortification, it will soon be better with you, and you will find peace. ... The more any one dies to himself, so much the more does he begin to live to God. ... Take always the lowest place and the highest will be given you, for the highest depends on the lowest. ... Without first humbling yourself, you will never ascend to heaven." Great is the sacrifice which is here required at the hands of man, being no less than inward annihilation and parting with all that is his own, but the requisition is immediately coupled with a promise as great, viz, that he shall receive God. God has given all to man, and desires that man may give himself back to the Giver, in order to receive God fully in return. Thomas puts the following language into the mouth of God, "My son, that thou mayest possess all, thou must wholly surrender thyself, reserving nothing. Forsake thyself and thou shalt find me. Have nothing of thine own, not even thy will, and great will be thy gain. Without the total abnegation of self, thou canst not attain perfect liberty. They who seek their own and love themselves are fettered slaves. Give then all for all, ask for nothing and require nothing back, continue wholly and steadfastly attached to me, and thou shalt possess me. Thou wilt be free in thy heart, and no darkness will cover thee. Let it be the aim of thy endeavors, prayers, and desires, to despoil thyself of all that is thine own, to follow Jesus naked as He was naked, to die to thyself, and live forever to me."

Here, however, we have already made the transition to the positive side of the matter. Not only must a man become free from the world, the creatures, and him-self, but God must also impart himself to him, in order that he may thenceforth live to God. The two things, however, being dependent upon each other, and tak-ing place simultaneously, cannot be effected by man alone, but are brought about essentially by God, and through divine grace. Man cannot by his own strength rise above his own level, and can only become participant of God by God's imparting himself to him, and infusing into him his spirit and his love. Having condensed his whole doctrine into the short rule, "Part with all and thou wilt find all," he im-mediately subjoins, "Lord, this is not the work of a day, nor a game for children. These few words include all perfection." Here, accordingly, an efficacy must in-tervene which is superior to human strength. This efficacy is divine love imparting itself to man, and becoming the mediatrix between God and him, between heaven and earth. Love brings together the holy God who dwells in heaven and the sinful creature upon earth, uniting that which is most humble with that which is most ex-alted. It is the truth that makes man free, but the highest truth is love. Divine love, imparting and manifesting itself to man, is grace. God sheds forth his love into the heart of man, who thereby acquires liberty, peace, and ability for all good things; and, made partaker of this love, man reckons as worthless all that is less than God, loving God only, and loving himself no more, or, if at all, only for God's sake. He loves all things in God, and is filled with the purest spirit of devotion, the most active zeal to do good. "Love," as Thomas in a sort of hymn pronounces her eu-logy, "love is truly a mighty good. It lightens the heaviest loads and smooths the inequalities of life. It bears the burden without feeling it, and gives sweetness and relish to the bitterest things. It prompts to great enterprises, and kindles the desire of higher and higher perfection. It aspires upward, and will not be restrained by the things of this earth. ... Nothing is sweeter than love, nothing stronger, nothing higher, nor more extensive, nor more pleasing, nor more full, nor more excellent in heaven or on earth, for love is born of God, and cannot find rest, but by rising above all created things to rest in God. It flies and runs, and is full of alacrity. It is free, and knows no restraint. It gives all for all, and possesses all in all, because it reposes in the one Supreme good, from which every good originates and flows. It regards not gifts, but rises above all blessings to Him who bestows them. It sees no difficulty, cares for no labor, and attempts what is above its strength. It complains not of impossibility, but looking upon all things as both possible and lawful, it has ability for all. Though exhausted it is never weary, though straitened not enslaved, and though alarmed not confounded; but, like a lively flame and burning torch, it darts upward, and forces a safe passage through every obstacle. ... Not that it is soft and fickle, or intent upon vain things, but strong, manly, prudent, circumspect, sober, chaste, steadfast, and calm, keeping a constant guard over the senses." He who has found love has found the best of things. "Love is of itself sufficient;" in it he possesses all that he can ever want. "Nothing is better for thee, nothing more salutary, nothing more pleasant, nothing worthier and higher, nothing more perfect and blessed, than most ardently to love and most highly to praise God. This I say a hundred times, and a thousand times do I repeat, do it as long as thou livest and possessest feeling and thought. Do it by word and deed, by day and by night, at morning, noon, and eve, every hour and every moment." True love to God, inasmuch as it springs from the renunciation of self, and the deepest sense of needing Him, likewise includes in it the purest humility; and humility is the fountain of wisdom and peace, more than lofty knowledge.

Love is the means of uniting the will of man with the will of God. He who loves God traces all things back to their first cause, and submits himself uncondi-tionally to his will; and what can impart a higher peace? "If you aim at and seek after that only which is well-pleasing to God, and profitable to your neighbor, you will enjoy inward peace. Every creature will be to you a mirror of life, and a book of sacred doctrine, and none of them so humble and vile, but will show forth to you the divine goodness." He who thus loves and whom love leads to devote himself to God, can say, "Lord, give me what thou wilt, and in what mea-sure, and at what time thou wilt. Deal with me as thou wilt, as thou seest to be best, as best pleaseth thee, and will best tend to thy honor. ... If it be thy will to leave me in darkness, blessed be thy name! Or if it be thy will that I should walk in thy light, blessed also be thy name! I desire to receive with indifference from thy hand, good and evil, sweet and bitter, joy and sorrow, and to be thankful for all that befalls me." In fine, divine love is also the means of restoring the right connection between man and man. It is not merely that henceforth we love men purely and freely in God, and for God's sake, and no more with a sensuous and creature-affection. But, moreover, all we have it in our power to do for them, all good works and virtues, thereby acquire their worth and importance. Love becomes not merely the incentive, but the very soul of virtue, that which first gives it its proper life. Without love the greatest achievement is nothing; but love makes the smallest great and divine. "Without the love of God and our neighbor," says Thomas, "no works are of any avail, even although they may be commended by men; they are but like empty vessels without oil, and lamps that give no light in the dark." And in another passage, "Without love no external work profiteth anything, but any work, however trifling and contemptible, if done from love, is fruitful; for God pays more regard to the disposition from which we act than to the amount we perform. He does much who loves much. He does much, who does well that which he does; and he does well that which he does who subserves the common good more than his own will. ... He who has true and perfect love does not seek himself in anything, but only desires that God may be glorified. He cares not to have joy in himself, but refers all to God, from whom, as their source, all blessings flow, and in whom, as their final end, all saints find a blissful repose."

It may excite surprise that in the whole preceding exposition, though mostly made up of quotations from Thomas's Imitation of Christ, no express mention is made of Christ's person. Although, however, not expressly, this has been implicitly done all the way; for he who names God and love has, according to the views of Thomas, also named Christ; and to speak of humility, self-denial, mortification, living in God, peace, and blessedness, is virtually to speak of Him. In Thomas's conception, Christ is the actual love of God manifested, uniting humanity with divinity; He is the prototype of perfect self-relinquishment and oneness with God, of unalterable peace and untroubled blessedness in God. His cross is the universal cross, his victory the victory of all the good who love God. The reception of Jesus into the heart is the reception of the divine love. Embracing there his passion and death, or, in other words, his cross, becomes the dying and crucifixion of self. The imitation of Jesus is the life of holy humility, self-denial, and affectionate labor for others. Hence the doctrine of the *Imitation of Christ* is of so great importance to Thomas, not merely in the book which bears that title, but generally in all his writings. Even in the smallest of his poems, it forms the leading thought.[22] Side by side with the fundamental maxim, "Give thyself wholly to God, and thou wilt wholly receive Him," stands another of no less weight, nay, substantially equivalent, "Receive Christ, let him be found within thee, follow him and imitate his example, and with him thou hast all." In Thomas's mind Christ no less than God, is the all in all, the Divine image, the pattern of the active as well as of the contemplative life, of how to act and how to suffer. He is the Master of all, the book and the rule of the religious, the model of the clergy, the doctrine of the laity, the text and commentary of the decrees, the light of believers, the rejoicing of the righteous, the praise of angels, the end and consummation of all the longing of the saints. How holy, then, the soul which wholly denies self, and molds its entire life into conformity with Christ! Christ sacrificed himself completely for us, and in his body and blood, is constantly imparting himself to us, in order that we may wholly become His, and continue to be so, and may live in him more than in ourselves. All others are to be loved for Jesus's sake, but Jesus, like God, for his own. He should be with us always, wherever we go, and dwell in us and walk with us. "If in all things thou seekest Jesus, thou wilt find him in them all. If in all things thou seekest thyself, thou wilt indeed find what thou seekest, but to thine own destruction." Above all, let Christ Crucified live in us, and His cross be wholly imprinted upon our hearts. To receive Christ crucified into the heart is the basis of all good. He pervades the whole inner man, and always and on every hand incites to good thoughts and deeds, fortifies timidity, drives away doubt, confirms faith, infuses love, and animates zeal. "In Christ the consummation of all the virtues beams forth as in a pure mirror, and in no book or science can anything better or more perfect be found or known than in this book of life, which is the true light.

---

22   Thomas expresses in poetry his thoughts on the Imitation of Christ, in the Vita boni Monachi, pp. 279 and 281, where two poems begin withthe words: Vitam Jesu Christi stude imitari.

But sweeter than incense is the perfume which the passion of my Master exhales, comprehending in it a compendium of all graces." And this passion or the cross of our Master principally teaches us, what elsewhere appears in Thomas's eyes, the sum of all virtue, viz., the surrender of our own will, obedience unto death, renunciation of the pleasures of the world, and cheerful patience in affliction.

According as Thomas apprehends the matter, Christ must be received into the heart, in a manner consistent with his nature and spirit, and must there take the place of the person's self. The image of Jesus, too, is always to be conceived in its totality, "He is to me, when I duly reflect upon the subject, whole and entire in particulars, nor does any difference of appearance or age change my belief of the truth, because Christ is undivided, and in all these forms equally to be adored." But we may, nevertheless, select the several points of his life and character, and hold them up to view. For in all these, we may find doctrine and example; and thus again Thomas uses the life of Christ, even to the minutest point, as a pattern for himself and others. In this respect he goes so far as to seek in Christ a precedent for transcribing books. In preaching upon that passage of the Gospel which tells us that Jesus "stooped down and with his finger wrote on the ground," he says, "It is pleasing to hear that Jesus could read and write, to the end that the art of writing and zeal in reading pious books may delight us the more. Take pleasure then in imitating Him, even in reading and writing, for it is a good, meritorious, and pious work to write such books as Jesus loves, and in which he is confessed and made known, and to keep them with the utmost care." In this manner, accordingly, a man may set the example of Christ before him in all the occurrences of life, and, at all times and in all respects, ought to mold himself into conformity with it, and according to the measure of human weakness, repeat Jesus in his own person.

It is true that dying to self, appropriating Christ, and becoming one with God, are generally represented by Thomas as a single act; but this is not to be understood as implying, that the operation is perfected in a single moment.[23] On the contrary, it embraces the entire being, and progresses to greater and greater perfection, through the whole course of life. Only by degrees, and under a lasting conflict, which, however, is ever more and more becoming victory and peace, can the inward death and the inward life be consummated. Contrition must still be renewed afresh, and mortification take place in ever larger measure. A man should extirpate a vice every year, and signalize every day and minute by an advancement in good, and some action calculated to please God. He should unite himself by an ever closer and closer approximation to God, until at length he is wholly dissolved and swallowed up in the divine love, and God within him, is one and all.

This explicative process, however dependent upon one decisive act of self-surrender and dedication to God, being nevertheless carried on gradually and in the face of difficulty and opposition, and never but disturbed by some alloy of sin, may yet be expedited by the use of certain means, and the adoption of a particular method of life. And here it is that Thomas brings in asceticism and makes the transition to monkery. While the sect of the Free Spirit taught that for the contemplative man all outward things are indifferent; and while Master Eckart advanced the dangerous tenet, that to such a man, the test of a thing's being good,

---

23   Non enim subita conversione, says Thomas of the apostles, whom he nevertheless contemplates as exemplars, nec una tantummodo die ad tam magnam verfectionen ascenderunt. Concio xxiii. de Spirit sancto, p. 249.

is merely his own inclination impelling to it, we find in Thomas the very opposite. He says, "No man is wholly secure from temptations, so long as he lives, for he has that which is the cause of them within himself." He teaches, "We must not believe every word we hear, nor follow every impulse; but we must cautiously and leisurely deliberate the matter in its relation to God…Take counsel of some prudent and conscientious man, and seek rather to be instructed by one who is better than yourself than to follow your own suggestions." He lays the whole stress upon breaking self-will: "The Cross consists in breaking self-will, and only the way of the Cross is the way of life." He everywhere insists upon a manful resistance to sensuality; upon guarding all the senses through which the temptation to evil may come, and, in order to enjoy solitude and sequestration in every place, upon building as it were a cell or tabernacle within one's own heart, and making in it but one window for the admission of Christ. It is only by closing the gates of sensuality that it is possible for a man to hear within him the word of the Lord, and calmly and collectedly to ponder on that which concerns his salvation. In order to bear up successfully in the conflict with sensuality and self, Thomas prescribes a series of religious and moral exercises, partly of a private and partly of a public kind. The private are, solitude, silence, fasting, prayer, reading and even copying the Scriptures and other useful books, submission to the direction of a superior, self-examination daily, and chiefly in the morning and at night, repeated recollection of God, eternity, heaven and hell, and unremitted occupation either of the body or the mind from the earliest to the latest hour of the day. The public are, regular attendance on divine worship, a zealous observance of all sacred rites and seasons, the faithful adoration of Mary and the saints, and a frequent participation of the Holy Supper. "Rise early, watch, pray, labor, read, write, be silent, sigh, and bravely endure all adversity;" these are Thomas's rules of life, which he never wearies of again and again repeating.

In this manner Thomas's religious views of things pass through the intermediate state of asceticism, and at last end in monachism. He shares the notion of almost the whole mediaeval period, in reckoning monachism the highest stage of the Christian life, and the monk the perfect Christian. This entailed two consequences: in the first place, much of a merely monkish nature mixes itself up in his mind with general Christianity, as we see even in the treatise of the "Imitation of Christ," which contains numerous passages calculated exclusively for monks, secondly, general Christian truth is viewed by him as the basis of monachism. This is shown in all his writings specially designed for monks, to whom in these he addresses the same religious and moral requirements as to every Christian, only superadding others of a higher kind. For the ideal which Thomas formed of monachism was certainly of no mean kind; here, as everywhere else, he evinces the same spirituality and rigor.

Trained ascetically from his youth up, Thomas was full of lively zeal for the monastic life. It is true that, prudent and gentle in his sentiments, he by no means wholly condemns life in the world. On the contrary, in a comparison, such as elsewhere is often found, of the contemplative life with Mary, and of the active with Martha, he admits that the part which Martha chose is also laudable and pleasing to God, and he insists that the sisters should not dispute to which the preference is due, but, mutually owning each other's advantages, unite in the common service of Christ. The part chosen by Mary, however, which here means the contemplative, and chiefly the cloisteral life, was to him the more eligible and pleasant, and he would have recommended every one to lead even the active life, rather in the cloister than in the world, which he considered quite practicable. In the same way Thomas also admits that it is not given to every one to forsake all, renounce the world, and embrace the monastic life; and it is for this reason that the devotees of contemplation are so few in number. At the same time, however, he expresses himself strongly against the men of the world attempting to restrain the young from entering the monastery, and refutes the objections current among them. Nowhere, as he thought, but in the cell, in which he felt himself so happy, could man be fully withdrawn from the world. The society of brethren living in one house, under the same governor, and according to the same rule, engaging in the same prayers, devotional exercises, and labor, and mutually encouraging and supporting each other in all things, appeared to him the most charming picture of the Christian life, and one nowhere else to be found. But from this point of view he also required much of the true monk and the proper monastery. "It is not the hood," he says, "which makes a monk, for it may be worn by an ass." All depends upon the inward frame of mind. As little had he any toleration for stupid and ignorant monks. "Woe," says he with severe rebuke, "to the clergyman without education or knowledge of the Scriptures, for he often becomes the occasion of error, both to himself and others! A clergyman without the Holy Scriptures is a soldier without weapons, a horse without a bridle, a ship without a rudder, a writer without a pen, and a bird without wings. And equally, a monastery which wants the Scriptures, is a kitchen without pots, a table without dishes, a well without water, a river without fish, a garden without flowers, a purse without money, and a house without furniture." Accordingly zeal for the study of Scripture, and some degree, however moderate, of theological education, are held by Thomas as indispensable requisites for the monastic clergyman. Still more so, however, did he reckon the Christian virtues, first those of a more general kind, which we have already detailed, and then the particular ones, which specially pertain to him. These are partly some of universal obligation upon monks, to wit, poverty, chastity, and obedience, and partly others more specific, such as humility, patience, silence, a fondness for solitude, self-contemplation, and entire mortification.[24] Religious poverty has in his eyes an equal value with martyrdom. He cannot sufficiently enforce the virtue of punctual obedience, to which he was himself inured from his youth up. Although he does not condemn wise and edifying conversation, silence appears to him always more advisable than speaking, solitude much more conducive to improvement than society, and prolonged abstraction and consideration of the things which promote contrition, the conditions of an ever-increasing fellowship with God.[25] Thomas further requires from the monk, as specially incumbent, a strictly methodical life, unintermitted activity, avoidance of all singularity, zeal in the social religious exercises, and affectionate activity for the common good of

---

24   Delineations of monastic life as it ought to be, and precepts and maxims for monks, may be found in all the works of Thomas. Vita boni Monachi in verses that rhyme, has, among other things, these lines:

> Sustine vim patiens. Tace, ut sis sapiens.
> Mores rege, aures tege. Saepe ora, saepe lege.
> Omni die, omni hora, te resigna, sine mora.

Translation.—"Sustain violence patiently. Be silent, that thou mayst be wise. Govern thy manners. Cover thy ears. Pray often, read often. Every day, every hour, be resigned, without delay."

25   Thomas has composed a particular treatise upon the salutary effects of solitude and silence. De Solitudine et Silentio, p. 225-242.

the brethren. He often gives summaries of the chief rules of the monastic life, of which we shall quote the two following instances: "Prompt obedience, frequent prayer, devout meditation, diligence in labor, fondness for study, the avoidance of conversation, and a relish for solitude—these are what make a good monk and give a peaceful mind." "The things which are above all necessary and profitable, both for a man's own advancement in virtue and for the edification of others, are solitude, silence, manual labor, prayer, reading, meditating upon the Scriptures, poverty, temperance, oblivion of one's native country, flying from the world, the quiet of a monastery, frequenting the choir, and remaining in the cell."[26] If we add the transcription of edifying books, we shall have mentioned all that Thomas was wont to recommend to monastic brethren.

Thomas was himself a rigid monk. He lays uncommon stress upon a strictly-regulated ascetical life,[27] speaks strongly against the luxury and pride of many monks, their pomp of dress, riches, and the costly architecture of their monasteries. He bestows most praise upon the strictest orders, to wit, the Carthusians and Cistercians, was himself punctual in all exercises, and used the scourge every week. Moderate in all other things, sensible of human weakness, and ever manifesting the innate gentleness of his disposition, he here disapproves of all extravagance and excess. Setting out from the principle, "that all which goes beyond measure and does not keep within its own distinctive limits, can neither please God nor he of long duration," he says, "If you wish to carry through a fixed method of life, you must steer a middle course between two extremes, so as not presumptuously to attempt what is above your ability, nor yet, on the other hand, slothfully to leave undone what you are well able to do. God requires of thee not the destruction of thy body, but the vanquishment of thy sins. He demands not what is unprofitable, but what is conducive to thy salvation. He counsels well, and provides the things necessary for thy life, in order that thou mayest make a good use of the body, to advance the welfare of the soul, but in no point to overstep the proper measure of discretion." "It is hence requisite in every spiritual work, in order to finish what you have well begun, to observe the common rule, to avoid singularity, in doubtful and dark points to follow the advice of the superior, and with the due measure of discrimination to yield obedience in all uprightness." In this manner, with temperance in meat and drink, and zeal in ascetic exercises, but without carrying them to an injurious extent, Thomas seems in his own case to have preserved to the last day of his life a healthy state of body and soul, a cheerful disposition, and a fresh and clear eye. It is also in part to be ascribed to the same moderation that he attained to so unusual an old age, whereas we behold Gerhard, Florentius, and Zerbolt, who, in the heat of conversion, gave themselves up to excessive penances, dying in early life.

We have thus sketched what is most essential in the views of Thomas. The reader may now ask with astonishment, shall this quiet mystic, wholly immersed in the contemplation of divine things, this recluse, obedient, rigidly Catholic monk, shall he be placed in the ranks of those who paved the way for the Reformation? We boldly answer in the affirmative. Thomas à Kempis was not, indeed, a precursor of the Reformation in the same sense as Wessel and others. He was not one in every respect; but he was so in several very weighty and important

---

26   "A monk out of his cell is a fish out of the water." Valley of Lilies, xviii. 1, p. 89.

27   The observance of discipline is to him of higher importance than the scientia Scripturarum, which he elsewhere s greatly values. De Discipl. Claustr., i. 2, p. 131.

aspects—we may even say with truth—in the core of his being.

It is true, Thomas was a strict Catholic, and directly impugned nothing which had received the sanction of the Church. He adhered strictly to the creed as it had been handed down, and did not assail the doctrines which generally have, and even in those days had, not unfrequently, excited opposition, and chiefly respected indulgences and transubstantiation; but rather expresses distinct assent to the latter. He practiced with great zeal the whole divine worship as it then obtained, and which as such appeared to him just what it ought to be, and insists with particular urgency upon what is so characteristically Catholic, prayers for the dead offered through the medium of the mass, especially the adoration of the saints, among whom he chiefly worships the patron-saints of his own monastery, and most of all the service of Mary, to whom he ascribes so important a share in the divine government of the world as to say of her, "How could a world, which is so full of sin endure unless Mary with the saints in Heaven were daily praying for it." He no less acknowledges the existing hierarchy and ecclesiastical constitution in their whole extent, together with the priesthood in its function of mediating between God, and man, and at least nowhere lifts his voice against the hierarchical corruptions and their oppressive effects, but on every occasion rather insists upon ecclesiastical obedience as one of the greatest virtues. The authority of the Church, accordingly, is, as regards him, wholly inviolate. His predominant principle is that of subjection and faith, so that he was disposed rather to bear any thing harsh and unjust, and embrace any thing untrue, as, for instance, imaginary miracles, than to excite opposition, or exercise criticism, which would have appeared to him in the light of infidel rashness.

It is no less true that the views of Thomas differed from the maturer form assumed by those of the Reformation in many not unimportant points. A taint of the pelagianism of the mediaeval theology manifestly enters into them, especially in those of his writings which are devoted to the delineation and recommendation of the monastic life, in which the notion of merit plays a not unimportant part. Like the generality of mystics, he occupies St. John's point of view more than that of St. Paul,[28] from which, however, the main impulse toward the Reformation proceeded. To him Christ is more the only-begotten of the Father, full of grace and of truth, the image of God, and the pattern of a life in and with God, than the author of atonement and redemption, and the Cross more the symbol of self-mortification than the memorial of Christ's sacrificial and mediatory death; and hence not justification by faith, but reconciliation by love, constitutes the center of his whole religious system. While Luther and men of like mind lay the main stress upon faith, and would hesitate to imperil its interests more than those of love, Thomas lays it upon love, and derives all good from that, and all evil from its opposite. With this principle of love, indeed, he connects, if not the whole legalism of the mediaeval Church, for which he was much too spiritual and free, still a certain measure of the traditional legality, inasmuch as he fences morality of life with a multitude of rules and exercises, and, especially in the case of the monk, subjects it to an outward bondage by no means in accordance with a truly evangelical spirit.

In spite of all this, however, we must maintain that between the childlike, humble Thomas, and the heroic and independent Luther, however diversely their

---

28   He therefore extols John in preference to the rest of the Apostles. Conoio i. de Incarn. Chr., p. 150.

physiognomies may contrast, there is yet a deep inward affinity, and that in the whole character of the former there exist reformatory elements in no inconsiderable measure. In proof of this it might be enough to view the matter upon its negative side, and the manner in which he treats religious subjects, although the positive is also of some importance.

Undoubtedly Thomas does not impugn any ecclesiastical dogma, but neither does he establish or defend any. With the dogma, as such, he does not meddle at all; but animates and enlivens it by his pious feelings. It is from the heart so to speak that he sets it in motion, employing it as the vehicle of his mysticism and asceticism. The interest he takes, however, is not so much in the doctrinal as in the moral. To the strict ecclesiastical orthodoxy of the reigning Catholicism, which was substantially represented by scholasticism, especially by Thomas Aquinas, his relation is little different from that in which the pietists stood to the Lutheran orthodoxy, under the scholastic form which it had assumed in the seventeenth century. Just as pietism, although fully adhering to the whole creed of the church, by the preponderating worth it assigned to practice in religion, brought about a certain indifference to strictness and precision of doctrine—a doctrinal latitudinarianism—which, in the sequel, although contrary to its desire, was transmuted into the rationalistic opposition, so the practical mysticism of the fifteenth century, as exhibited by the Brethren of the Common Lot, the pietists of Catholicism, and especially by Thomas à Kempis, produced a similar effect. The only difference was, that on the overthrow of the creed in the Protestant Church, abstract intellect ascended the throne; whereas, in the other case, the heart of mysticism continued to operate in the new theological creation of the Reformers. Scholasticism and mysticism, as we find them in the fifteenth century, had wholly changed their original positions. At first, in the twelfth century, mysticism was preeminently the chief defender of the Church, as for instance is evinced by Bernard's contest with Abelard; afterward scholasticism in its principal representatives had entirely devoted itself to the Church's cause, and become, properly speaking, the legitimate theology. This place it occupied in the fifteenth century, whereas on the contrary the elements of opposition were for the most part upon the side of mysticism; and inasmuch as à Kempis also belongs to that side, inasmuch as he is manifestly anti-scholastical, gives prominence solely to the religious and moral import of the dogma, and applies it almost exclusively to the use of the mystical and ascetical life, we must, from a regard to his edifying character, ascribe to him a real, although an indirect, influence in the dissolution of the creed. Another proof of the little interest he took in the ecclesiastical doctrine is afforded by the circumstance that he never turns his arms against errors in faith. He makes war, not with heretics but with the world. In his eyes sin is the great heresy, and the object of continual hostility. Nor has he the narrow-mindedness necessarily pertaining to a rigid dogmatist of his Church. "Jesus," as he beautifully says, "is not always to be found in the place where we seek Him, but is often in the place where we least expect Him. Let no one presume that Christ belongs solely to him. Let no one despise his neighbor, for he cannot tell how far he may secretly be acceptable to God, although apparently unknown and contemptible in the sight of men. Jesus himself was once unknown to the multitude, and few perceived who and how great He was."

Such was the position of Thomas as a doctrinalist; and similar was that which he occupied with reference to the rites of religious worship. Here, also, he was faithful, happy, and conscientious in practicing the received forms. But here also it is not the ecclesiastical work itself, the *opus operatum*, which has a value in his eyes, but the disposition with which it is performed, the faith and love which it manifests, and which, in their turn, receive from it nourishment and vigor. It is the all-pervading soul of piety to which he invariably looks, and on which he sets a value. This view he admirably expresses in an opinion respecting the festivals of the Church. "No festival is a festival for me which is not celebrated in the heart, and the only reason for its frequent outward repetition is, that it may be inwardly kept with the greater heartiness and joy. Outward festivals are only a means of incitement to those within, and a foretaste of everlasting joys…All our festivals are rather preludes to the festival of eternity, than deserving the name of festivals in themselves. Here they are only begun in the light of faith; there, however, they are consummated in the light of glory."

In fine, just as little did he assail the hierarchy; in general it is an object of no attention to him. He lets it stand, and passes it by in silence. The whole outward structure of the church is for him as if it had no existence; he cleaves to the living spirit within it, and to that alone. In his numerous writings he does not so much as mention the Pope by name, and only once alludes to him for the purpose of saying, that even he, a mortal man, and his leaden bull, like all earthly objects, are nothing.[29] Had it been his lot ever to hold intercourse with a pope, especially with any of the immoral ones of the fifteenth century, he would, like St. Bernard, have exhorted him to repentance, self-denial, and the renunciation of earthly things. The secularization of the Church, so far as he was acquainted with it, must have been to one who had so little of a worldly spirit as Thomas, an abomination. All he did and thought was based upon the saying of Christ, "My kingdom is not of this world," and from that point of view he could not but also contemplate the Church. Hence he speaks against striving after honors either academical or ecclesiastical, against the wealth of churches and monasteries, simony, plurality of ecclesiastical offices, and the secularities of monachism.

But all this, how opposite soever the spirit it evinces to the prevalent reverence for the Church, is rather of a negative character. We have to point to certain particulars more important and positive. In the first place, Thomas everywhere insists upon the Christian principles of spirituality and freedom, which formed the basis of the Reformation. Besides, the spirit of his fraternity led him to do many things involved in the general current which brought about the Reformation. To him the inward life, the disposition of mind, is the great matter. No work or external thing is of any value except through love. Where there is genuine love, it sanctifies all. In like manner he knows nothing more exalted than freedom. Freedom of mind is in his eyes the supreme good in the spiritual life. To be detached from all creatures, dependent only upon God, but in this dependence perfectly master of one's self and of all other things, this is to him the great mark, which the spiritual man ought to strive to reach. It is true that Thomas is not intentionally a Reformer, for he does not apply these principles outwardly. But he nevertheless is a

---

29   Sapiens est ille, qui spernit millia mille.
       Omnia sunt nulla, Rex, Papa et plumbea bulla.
       Cunctorum finis; mors, vermis, fovea, cinis.
    See Hortul. Rosar iv. 3. With which connect Vallis Iilior. xxv. 3: Nemo unius diei certitudinem vivendi habet, nec impetrare potest a Papa bullam nunquam moriendi, nec obtinere pecunia praebendam jugiter manontem, etc.

Reformer; for he desired the self-same objects as Luther and his friends, the only difference being that the latter also prosecuted them to their outward consequences. But besides, in the spirit of the fraternity of which he was a member, Thomas did many things to pave the way for reform. These consisted chiefly in zealously inculcating the reading of the Bible, and the transcription of copies of it, a work in which he himself took an active part—in laying the chief weight not upon Moses or any sort of law, but upon Christ and his Gospel, upon grace, repentance, faith, love, and the appropriation of the spirit of Scripture by the Spirit of God in the soul—in laboring much for the religious revival and instruction of the people by sermons and collationes—and in practically evincing a lively concern for the literary, and especially the philological, education of the rising generations. All this included the germ of future evolutions, although the harvest which they bore was such as Thomas never anticipated, and, if foreshown to him, would scarcely have recognized as the growth of his own seed.

THE IMITATION
OF
CHRIST

BOOK ONE

PREPARATORY INSTRUCTIONS
FOR THE SPIRITUAL LIFE.

I. CONTEMPT OF WORLDLY VANITIES.

"He that followeth me shall not walk in darkness, but shall have the light of life." These are the words of Christ; by which we are taught, that it is only by a conformity to his life and spirit that we can be truly enlightened, and delivered from all blindness of heart: let it, therefore, be the principal employment of our minds to meditate on the life of Christ.

The doctrine of Christ infinitely transcends the doctrine of the holiest men; and he that had the Spirit of Christ would find in it "hidden manna, the bread that came down from heaven:" but not having His Spirit, many, though they frequently hear his doctrine, yet feel no pleasure in it, no ardent desire after it; for he only can cordially receive, and truly delight in the doctrine of Christ, who continually endeavors to acquire the spirit and imitate the life of Christ.

Of what benefit are thy most subtle disquisitions into the mystery of the blessed Trinity, if thou art destitute of humility, and, therefore, a profaner of the Trinity? It is not profound speculations, but a holy life that proves a man righteous and good. I had rather feel compunction than be able to give the most accurate definition of it. If thy memory could retain the whole Bible, and the precepts of all the philosophers, what would it profit thee without charity and the grace of God! "Vanity of vanities! and all is vanity," except only the love of God, and an entire devotedness to His service.

It is the highest wisdom, by the contempt of the world, to press forward toward the kingdom of heaven. It is therefore vanity to labor for perishing riches, and place our confidence in their possession: it is vanity to hunt after honors, and raise ourselves to an exalted station: it is vanity to fulfill the lusts of the flesh, and indulge desires that begin and end in torment: it is vanity to wish that life may be long, and to have no concern whether it be good: it is vanity to mind only the present world, and not to look forward to that which is to come: to suffer our affections to hover over a state in which all things pass away with the swiftness of thought, and not raise them to that where true joy abideth forever.

Frequently call to mind the observation of Solomon, that "the eye is not satisfied with seeing, nor the ear filled with hearing;" and let it be thy continual endeavor to withdraw thy heart from the love of "the things that are seen," and to turn it wholly to "the things that are not seen;" for he who lives in subjection to the sensual desires of animal nature defiles his spirit, and loses the grace of God.

II. HUMILITY WITH RESPECT TO INTELLECTUAL ATTAINMENTS.

Every man naturally desires to increase in knowledge; but what doth knowledge profit without the fear of the Lord? Better is the humble clown that serveth God than the proud philosopher who, destitute of the knowledge of himself, can describe the course of the planets. He that truly knows himself becomes vile in his own eyes, and has no delight in the praise of man. If I knew all that the world contains, and had not charity, what would it avail me in the sight of God who will judge me according to my deeds?

Rest from an inordinate desire of knowledge, for it is subject to much perplexity and delusion. Learned men are fond of the notice of the world, and desire to be accounted wise: but there are many things the knowledge of which has no tendency to promote the recovery of our first divine life; and it is surely a proof of folly to devote ourselves wholly to that with which our supreme good has no connection. The soul is not to be satisfied with the multitude of words; but a holy life is a continual feast, and a pure conscience the foundation of a firm and immovable confidence in God. The more thou knowest, and the better thou understandest, the more severe will be thy condemnation, unless thy life be proportionably more holy. Be not, therefore, exalted for any uncommon skill in any art or science; but let the superior knowledge that is given thee make thee more fearful, and more watchful over thyself. If thou supposest that thou knowest many things, and hast perfect understanding of them, consider how many more things there are which thou knowest not at all; and, instead of being exalted with a high opinion of thy great knowledge, be rather abased by an humble sense of thy much greater ignorance. And why dost thou prefer thyself to another, since thou mayest find many who are more learned than thou art, and better instructed in the will of God?

The highest and most profitable learning is the knowledge and contempt of ourselves; and to have no opinion of our own merit, and always to think well and highly of others, is an evidence of great wisdom and perfection. Therefore, though thou seest another openly offend, or even commit some enormous sin, yet thou must not from thence take occasion to value thyself for thy superior goodness; for thou canst not tell how long thou wilt be able to persevere in the narrow path of virtue. All men are frail, but thou shouldst reckon none so frail as thyself.

III. KNOWLEDGE OF THE TRUTH.

Blessed is the man whom eternal Truth teacheth, not by obscure figures and transient sounds, but by direct and full communication! The perceptions of our senses are narrow and dull, and our reasoning on those perceptions frequently misleads us. To what purpose are our keenest disputations on hidden and obscure subjects, for our ignorance of which we shall not be brought into judgment at the great day of universal retribution? How extravagant the folly to neglect the study of the "one thing needful;" and wholly devote our time and faculties to that which is not only vainly curious, but sinful and dangerous as the state of "those that have eyes and see not!"

What have redeemed souls to do with the distinctions and subtleties of logical divinity? He whom the eternal Word condescendeth to teach is disengaged at once from the labyrinth of human opinions. For "of one word are all things;" and all things without voice or language speak Him alone: He is that divine principle which speaketh in our hearts; and, without which, there can be neither just apprehension nor rectitude of judgment. Now, He to whom all things are but this one; who comprehendeth all things in His will, and beholdeth all things in His light; hath "his heart fixed," and abideth in the peace of God. O God, who art the truth, make me one with Thee in everlasting love! I am often weary of reading, and weary of hearing: in Thee alone is the sum of my desire! Let all teachers be silent, let the whole creation be dumb before Thee, and do Thou only speak unto my soul!

The more a man is devoted to internal exercises, and advanced in singleness and simplicity of heart, the more sublime and diffusive will be his knowledge. A spirit pure, simple, and constant, is not like Martha, "distracted and troubled with the multiplicity of its employments," however great; because, being inwardly at rest, it seeketh not its own glory in what it does, but "doth all to the glory of God:" for there is no other cause of perplexity and disquiet, but an unsubdued will and unmortified affections. A holy and spiritual mind, by reducing them to the rule and standard of his own mind, becomes the master of all his outward acts; he does not suffer himself to be led by them to the indulgence of inordinate affections that terminate in self, but subjects them to the unalterable judgment of an illuminated and sanctified spirit.

No conflict is so severe as his who labors to subdue himself; but in this we must be continually engaged, if we would be strengthened in the inner man, and make real progress toward perfection. Indeed, the highest perfection we can attain to in the present state is alloyed with much imperfection, and our best knowledge is obscured by the shades of ignorance; "we see through a glass darkly:" an humble knowledge of thyself, therefore, is a more certain way of leading thee to God than the most profound investigations of science. Science, however, or a proper knowledge of the things that belong to the present life, is so far from being blamable considered in itself, that it is good, and ordained of God; but purity of conscience, and holiness of life, must ever be preferred before it; and because men are more solicitous to learn much than to live well, they fall into error, and receive little or no benefit from their studies. But if the same diligence was exerted to eradicate vice and implant virtue, as is applied to the discussion of unprofitable questions, and the "vain strife of words;" so much daring wickedness would not be found among the common ranks of men, nor so much licentiousness disgrace those who are eminent for knowledge. Assuredly, in the approaching day of universal judgment, it will not be inquired what we have read, but what we have done; not how eloquently we have spoken, but how holily we have lived.

Tell me, where is now the splendor of those learned doctors and professors, whom, while the honors of literature were blooming around them, you so well knew, and so highly reverenced? Their emoluments and offices are possessed by others, who scarcely have them in remembrance: the tongue of fame could speak of no name but theirs while they lived, and now it is utterly silent about them: so suddenly passeth away the glory of human attainments! Had these men been as solicitous to be holy as they were to be learned, their studies might have been blessed with that honor which can not be sullied, and that happiness which can not be interrupted. But many are wholly disappointed in their hopes both of honor and happiness, by seeking them in the pursuit of "science falsely so called;" and not in the knowledge of themselves, and the life and service of God: and choosing rather to be great in the eyes of men, than meek and lowly in the sight of God, they become vain in their imaginations, and their memorial is written in the dust.

He is truly good, who hath great charity; he is truly great, who is little in his own estimation, and rates at nothing the summit of worldly honor: he is truly wise, who "counts all earthly things but as dross, that he may win Christ:" and he is truly learned, who hath learned to abandon his own will, and do the will of God.

IV. PRUDENCE WITH RESPECT TO OPINIONS AND ACTIONS.

We must not believe every word we hear, nor trust the suggestions of every spirit; but consider and examine all things with patient attention, and in reference to God; for so great, alas! is human frailty, that we are more ready to believe and speak evil of one another than good. But a holy man is not forward to give credit to the reports of others; because, being sensible of the darkness and malignity of nature, he knows that it is prone to evil, and too apt to pervert truth in the use of speech. It is an evidence of true wisdom, not to be precipitate in our actions, nor inflexible in our opinions; and it is a part of the same wisdom, not to give hasty credit to every word that is spoken, nor immediately to communicate to others what we have heard, or even what we believe. In cases of perplexity and doubt, consult a prudent and religious man; and choose rather to be guided by the counsel of one better than thyself, than to follow the suggestions of thy own blind will.

A holy life, however, makes a man wise according to the divine wisdom, and wonderfully enlarges his experience. The more humble his spirit is, and the more subject and resigned to God, the more wise will he become in the conduct of outward life, and the more undisturbed in the possession of himself.

V. READING THE SCRIPTURES AND OTHER HOLY BOOKS.

Not eloquence, but truth, is to be sought in the holy Scriptures, every part of which must be read with the same spirit by which it was written. In these, and all other books, it is improvement in holiness, not pleasure in the subtlety of thought, or the accuracy of expression, that must be principally regarded. We ought to read those parts that are simple and devout, with the same affection and delight as those of high speculation, or profound erudition. Whatever book thou readest, suffer not thy mind to be influenced by the character of the writer, whether his literary accomplishments be great or small. Let thy only motive to read be the love of truth; and, instead of inquiring who it is that writes, give all thy attention to the nature of what is written. Men pass away like the shadows of the morning; but "the word of the Lord endureth forever:" and that word, without respect of persons, in ways infinitely various, speaketh unto all.

The profitable reading of the holy Scriptures is frequently interrupted by a vain curiosity which prompts us to examine, discuss, and labor to comprehend those parts that should be meekly and submissively passed over. But to derive spiritual improvement from reading, we must read with humility, simplicity, and faith and not affect the reputation of profound learning.

VI. INORDINATE AFFECTIONS.

The moment a man gives way to inordinate desire, disquietude and torment take possession of his heart. The proud and the covetous are never at rest; but the humble and poor in spirit, possess their souls in the plenitude of peace.

He that is not perfectly dead to himself, is soon tempted and easily subdued, even in the most ordinary occurrences of life. The weak in spirit who is yet carnal, and inclined to the pleasures of sense, finds great difficulty in withdrawing himself from earthly desires; he feels regret and sorrow, as often as this abstraction is attempted; and every opposition to the indulgence of his ruling passion, kindles his indignation and resentment. If he succeeds in the gratification of inordinate desire, he is immediately stung with remorse; for he has not only contracted the guilt of sin, but is wholly disappointed of the peace which he sought. It is, therefore, not by indulging, but by resisting our passions, that true peace of heart is to be found. It can not be the portion of him that is carnal, nor of him that is devoted to a worldly life; it dwells only with the humble and the spiritual.

VII. VAIN HOPE AND ELATION OF MIND.

He that placeth his confidence in man, or in any created being, is vain, and trusteth in a shadow. Be not ashamed to serve thy brethren in the meanest offices, and to appear poor in the sight of men, for the love of Jesus Christ. Presume not upon the success of thine own endeavors, but place all thy hope in God; do all that is in thy power with an upright intention, and God will bless with his favor the integrity of thy will. Trust not in thy own wisdom, nor in the wisdom and skill of any human being; but trust in the grace and favor of God, who raises the humble, and humbles the presuming.

Glory not in riches, though they increase upon thee; nor in friends, because they are powerful, but glory in God, who giveth riches, and friends, and all things. Be not vain of the gracefulness, strength, and beauty of thy body, which a little sickness can weaken and deform. Please not thyself with flattering reflections on the acuteness of thy natural understanding, and the sweetness of thy natural disposition, lest thou displease God, who is the Author of all the good that nature can dispense. Do not think thou art better than others, lest, in the sight of God, who only knoweth what is in man, thou be found worse. Be not proud of that in which thou art supposed to excel, however honored and esteemed by men; for the judgment of God and the judgment of men are infinitely different, and that displeaseth him which is commonly pleasing to them. Whatever good thou art truly conscious of, think more highly of the good of others, that thou mayst preserve the humility of thy spirit: to place thyself lower than all mankind, can do thee no hurt; but much hurt may be done, by preferring thyself to a single individual. Perpetual peace dwelleth with the humble, but envy, indignation, and wrath, distract the heart of the proud.

VIII. INTERCOURSE WITH THE WORLD.

"Open not thine heart to every man;" but intrust its secrets to him only that is wise, and feareth God. Be seldom in the company of young men and strangers. Flatter not the rich; nor affect to be seen the presence of the great. Associate chiefly with the humble and simple, the holy and devout; and let thy conversation with them be on subjects that tend to the perfection of thy spirit. Wish to be familiar with God, and his holy angels, but shun the notice and intimacy of men; charity is due to all, but familiarity is the right of non.

It often happens, that a stranger, whom the voice of fame had made illustrious, loses the brightness of his character, the moment he is seen and known: we hope to please others by entering into familiar connections with them; and we presently disgust them, by the evil qualities and irregular behavior which they discover in us.

IX. SUBJECTION AND OBEDIENCE.

It is more beneficial to live in subjection than in authority; and to obey is safer than to command. Many live in subjection, more from necessity than the love of God; and, therefore, pass a life of continual labor, and find occasion to murmur in the most trifling events: nor can they possibly acquire liberty of spirit, until, with the whole heart, they are resigned, in all situations, to the will of God. Go where thou wilt, rest is not to be found, but in humble submission to the Divine will. A fond imagination of being easier in any place than that which Providence has assigned us, and a desire of change grounded upon it, are both deceitful and tormenting.

Men love to act from their own judgment, and are most inclined to those that are of the same opinion with themselves. But if God dwell in our hearts, we shall find it necessary frequently to abandon our own sentiments, for the sake of peace. And who is so perfectly wise as to comprehend the causes and connections of all things? Be not too confident, therefore, in thy own judgment, but willingly hearken to the judgment of others. And though in a question of speculative knowledge, or a case of worldly prudence, thy own opinion may be good; yet if, for the sake of God, thou canst quietly relinquish it, and submit to the opinion of another, it will greatly conduce to thy spiritual perfection. I have often heard, that it is more safe to take advice, than to give it. In some instances, it may happen, that each man's opinion may be so equally good, as to produce suspension on both sides, rather than submission on either; but to refuse submission to the opinion of another, when truth or the circumstances of the case require it, is a proof of a proud and pertinacious spirit.

X. SUPERFLUOUS TALKING.

As much as lies in thy power, shun the resorts of worldly men; for much conversation on secular business, however innocently managed, greatly retards the progress of the spiritual life. We are soon captivated by vain objects and employments, and soon defiled; and I have wished a thousand times that I had either not been in company, or had been silent.

If it be asked, Why we are so fond of mixing in the familiar and unprofitable conversations of the world, from which we so seldom return to silence and recollection without defilement and compunction, it must be answered, Because we seek all our consolation in the present life, and therefore hope, by the amusements of company, to efface the impressions of sorrow; and because of those things that we most love and desire, and of those that we most hate and would avoid, we are fond of thinking and speaking. But, alas! how deceitful is this artificial management! for the hope of consolation from outward life, utterly destroys that inward and divine consolation which the Holy Spirit gives us, and which is the only support of the soul under all its troubles. Let us, therefore, watch and pray without ceasing, that no part of our invaluable time may be thus sacrificed to vanity and sin: and whenever it is proper and expedient to speak, let us speak those things that are holy, by which Christians "edify one another."

An evil habit of negligence and inattention to our growth in grace, is the principal cause of our keeping no guard upon our lips. Spiritual conferences, however, are highly serviceable to spiritual improvement, especially when persons of one heart and one mind associate together in the fear and love of God.

XI. PEACE OF MIND, AND ZEAL FOR IMPROVEMENT.

We might enjoy much peace if we did not busy our minds with what others do and say in which we have no concern. But how is it possible for that man to dwell long in peace who continually intermeddles in the affairs of another who runs abroad seeking occasions of disquietude, and never or but seldom turns to God in the retirement of a recollected spirit? Blessed are the meek and single-hearted, for they shall possess the abundance of peace!

Whence was it that some of the saints became so perfect in the prayer of contemplation, but because it was their continual study and endeavor to mortify earthly desires, and abstract themselves from worldly concerns, that being free from perturbation, they might adhere to God with all the powers of the soul? But we are too much engaged with our own passions, and too tenderly affected by the business and pleasures of this transitory life, to be capable of such high attainments, nay, so fixed are our spirits in slothfulness and cold indifference that we seldom overcome so much as one evil habit.

If we were perfectly dead to ourselves, and free from all inward entanglement, we might have some relish for divine enjoyments, and begin to experience the blessedness of heavenly contemplation. The principal, if not the only impediment to such a state is, that we continue in subjection to violent passions and inordinate desires without making effort to enter into the narrow way, which Christ has pointed out as the one way of perfection for all the saints of God. Therefore, when adversity comes upon us, we are soon dejected, and have immediate recourse to human consolations. Did we but endeavor, like valiant soldiers, to stand our ground in the hour of battle, we should feel the succor of the Lord descending upon us from Heaven: for He is always ready to assist those that resolutely strive, and place their whole confidence in the power of His grace, nay, He creates occasions of contest to bless us with opportunities of victory.

If the progress to perfection is placed only in external observances, our religion, having no divine life, will quickly perish with the things on which it subsists; the ax must be laid to the root of the tree, that being separated and freed from the restless desires of nature and self, we may possess our souls in the peace of God. If every year we did but extirpate one vice, we should soon become perfect men: but some experience the sad reverse of this, and find that they were more contrite, more pure, more humble, and obedient, in the beginning of their conversion than after many years profession of a religious life. It would be but reasonable to expect that the fervor of our affections, and our progress in holiness, should advance higher and higher every day: but it is by some thought to be a foundation of comfort, and even of boast, if a man, at the close of this mortal state, is able to retain some degree of his first ardor.

That the path of holiness may become easy and delightful, some violence must be used at first setting out to remove its numerous obstructions. It is hard, indeed, to relinquish that to which we have been accustomed, and harder still to resist and deny our own will. But how can we hope to succeed in the greatest conflict if we will not contend for victory in the least? Resist, then, thy inordinate desires in their birth; and continually lessen the power of thy evil habits, lest they increase in strength in proportion as they are indulged, and grow at length too mighty to be subdued. O! if thou didst but consider what peace thou wilt bring to thyself, and what joy thou wilt produce in Heaven, by a life conformed to the life of Christ, I think thou wouldst be more watchful and zealous for thy continued advancement toward spiritual perfection.

XII. THE BENEFIT OF ADVERSITY.

It is good for man to suffer the adversity of this earthly life; for it brings him back to the sacred retirement of the heart, where only he finds that the heart is an exile from his native home, and ought not to place his trust in any worldly enjoyment. It is good for him also to meet with contradiction and reproach; to be evil thought of, and evil spoken of, even when his intentions are upright, and his actions blameless; for this keeps him humble, and is a powerful antidote to the poison of vain-glory. When we are outwardly despised, and held in no degree of esteem and favor among men, then chiefly it is that we have recourse to the witness within us, which is God. Our dependence upon God ought to be so entire and absolute that we should never think it necessary, in any kind of distress, to have recourse to human consolations.

When a regenerate man is sinking under adversity, or disturbed and tempted by evil thoughts, then he feels the necessity of the power and presence of God in his soul, without which he certainly knows that he can neither bear evil nor do good; then he grieves and prays, and "groans to be delivered from the bondage of corruption;" then weary of living in vanity, he wishes to "die, that he may be dissolved, and be with Christ;" and then he is fully convinced that absolute security and perfect rest are not compatible with his present state of life.

XIII. TEMPTATIONS.

As long as we continue in this world, we can not possibly be free from the trouble and anguish of temptation. In confirmation of this truth, it is written in Job that "the life of man upon earth is a continual warfare." Every one, therefore, ought to be attentive to the temptations that are peculiar to his own spirit; and to persevere in watchfulness and prayer, lest his "adversary the devil, who never sleepeth, but continually goeth about, seeking whom he may devour," should find some unguarded place where he may enter with his delusions.

The highest degree of holiness attainable by man is no security against the assaults of temptation, from which his present life is not capable of absolute exemption. But temptations, however dangerous and afflicting, are highly beneficial, because, under their discipline we are humbled, purified, and led toward perfection. All the followers of Christ have, through "much tribulation and affliction, entered into the kingdom of God;" and those that could not endure the trial, have "fallen from the faith and expectation of the saints, and become reprobate."

There is no order of men, however holy, nor any place, however secret and remote, where and among whom temptations will not come for the exercise of meekness, and troubles rise for the trial of patient resignation. And that this must be the condition of human nature in the present life is evident, because it is born in sin, and contains in itself those restless and inordinate desires which are the ground of every temptation: so that when one temptation is removed, another succeeds; and we shall always have some degree of evil to suffer, till we recover the purity and perfection of that state from which we have fallen.

Many, by endeavoring to fly from temptations have fallen precipitately into them; for it is not by flight, but by patience and humility, that we must become superior to all our enemies. He who only declines the outward occasion, and strives not to eradicate the inward principle, is so far from conquest, that the temptation will recur the sooner, and with greater violence, and he will feel the conflict still more severe. It is by gradual advances, rather than impetuous efforts, that victory is obtained; rather by patient suffering that looks up to God for support, than by impatient solicitude and rigorous austerity.

In thine own temptations, often ask counsel of those that have been tried, and have overcome; and in the temptations of thy brother, treat him not with severity, but tenderly administer the comfort which you desire to receive.

That which renders the first assaults of temptation peculiarly severe and dangerous, is the instability of our own minds, arising from the want of faith in God; and as a ship without a steersman, is driven about by the force of contrary winds, so an unstable man, that has no faith in God, is tossed and borne away upon the wave of every temptation.

"Gold is tried in the fire, and acceptable men in the furnace of adversity." We frequently know not the strength that is hidden in us, till temptation calls it forth, and shows us how much we are able to sustain. We must not, however, presume, but be particularly upon our guard against the first assaults; for the enemy will be more easily subdued, if he is resisted in his approaches, and not suffered to enter the portal of our hearts. A certain poet gives this advice:

> "Take physic early; medicines come too late,
> When the disease is grown inveterate."

And the caution may be successfully applied to the assaults of sin, the progress of which is gradual and dangerous. Evil is at first presented to the mind by a single suggestion; the imagination kindled by the idea, seizes it with strength, and feeds upon it; this produces sensual delight, then the motions of inordinate desire, and at length the full consent of the will. Thus, the malignant enemy, not resisted in his first attack, enters by gradual advances, and takes entire possession of the heart: and the longer opposition is deferred by habitual negligence, the power of opposing becomes every day less, and the strength of the adversary proportionably greater.

To some, temptations are more severe at the beginning of their religious course; to others, at the end: some are afflicted with them during the whole of life; and some experience comparatively short and gentle trials. This variety is adjusted by the wisdom and equity of divine Providence, which hath weighed the different states and dispositions of men, and ordered all its dispensations so as most effectually to tend to the salvation of all. Therefore, when we are tempted, let us not despair; but rather, with more animated fervors of faith, hope, and love, pray to God that he would vouchsafe to support us under all our trials, and, in the language of St. Paul, "with every temptation, to make also a way to escape," that we may be able to bear it. "Let us humble our souls, under the hand of God," who hath promised to "save and exalt the lowly and the meek."

By these trials, proficiency in the Christian life is proved. The power of divine grace is more sensibly felt in ourselves, and the fruits of it are more illustriously apparent to others. It is, indeed, a little matter, for a man to be holy and devout, when he feels not the pressure of any evil: but if, in the midst of troubles, he maintains his faith, his hope, his resignation, and "in patience possesses his soul," he gives a considerable evidence of a regenerate nature. Some, however, who have been blest with victory in combating temptations of the most rigorous kind, are yet suffered to fall even by the lightest that arise in the occurrences of daily life; that being humbled by the want of power to resist such slight attacks, they may never presume upon their own strength to repel those that are more severe.

XIV. RASH JUDGMENT.

Keep thy eye turned inwardly upon thyself, and beware of judging the actions of others. In judging others, a man labors to no purpose, commonly errs, and easily sins: but in examining and judging himself, he is always wisely and usefully employed.

We generally judge of persons and things as they either oppose or gratify our private views and inclinations; and, blinded by self-love, are easily led from the judgment of truth. If God alone was the pure object of all our intentions and desires, we should not be troubled when the truth of things happens to be repugnant to our own sentiments: but now, we are continually drawn aside from truth and peace, by some partial inclination lurking within, or some apparent good or evil rising without.

Many, indeed, secretly seek themselves in every thing they do, and perceive it not. These, while the course of things perfectly coincides with the sentiments and wishes of their own hearts, seem to possess all the blessings of peace; but when their wishes are disappointed, and their sentiments opposed, they are immediately disturbed, and become wretched.

From the diversity of inclinations and opinions tenaciously adhered to, arise dissensions among friends and countrymen, nay, even among the professors of a religious and holy life.

It is difficult to extirpate that which custom has deeply rooted; and no man is willing to be carried further than his own inclinations and opinions lead him. If, however, thou adherest more to thy own reason and thy own will, than to the meek obedience of Jesus Christy as the principle of all virtue within thee; thou wilt but slowly, if ever, receive the illuminations of the Holy Spirit. For God expects an entire and absolute subjection of our will to his; and that the flames of divine love should infinitely transcend the sublimest heights of human reason.

XV. WORKS OF CHARITY.

Let not the hope of any worldly advantage, nor the affection thou bearest to any creature, prevail upon thee to do that which is evil. For the benefit of him, however, who stands in need of relief, a customary good work may sometimes be intermitted; for, in such a case, that good work is not annihilated, but incorporated with a better.

Without charity, that is love, the external work profiteth nothing; but whatever is done from charity, however trifling and contemptible in the opinion of men, is wholly fruitful in the acceptance of God, who regardeth more the degree of love with which we act, than what or how much we have performed. He doeth much, who loveth much; he doeth much, who doth well; and he doth much and well, who constantly preferreth the good of the community to the gratification of his own will. Many actions, indeed, assume the appearance of charity, that are wholly selfish and carnal; for inordinate affection, self-will, the hope of reward, and the desire of personal advantage and convenience, are the common motives that influence the conduct of men.

He that has true and perfect charity, "seeketh not his own" in any thing, but seeketh only that "God may he glorified in all things;" he "envieth not," for he desires no private gratification: he delights not in himself, nor in any created being; but wishes for that which is infinitely transcendent, to be blest in the enjoyment of God: he ascribes not good to any creature, but refers it absolutely to God: from whom, as from its fountain, all good originally flows; in whom, as in their center, all saints will finally rest.

XVI. BEARING THE INFIRMITIES OF OTHERS.

Those evils which a man can not rectify, he ought to bear with humble resignation, till God shall be pleased to produce a change. This state of imbecility is, perhaps, continued, as the proper trial of patience, without the perfect work of which, we shall make but slow and ineffectual progress in the Christian life. Yet, under these impediments, we must devoutly pray, that God would enable us, by the assistance of his Spirit, to bear them with constancy and meekness.

If "after the first and second admonition, thy brother will not obey the truth," contend no longer with him; but leave the event to God, who only knoweth how to turn evil into good, that his will may be done, and his glory accomplished in all his creatures.[30]

Endeavor to be always patient of the faults and imperfections of others: for thou hast many faults and imperfections of thy own, that require a reciprocation of forbearance. If thou art not able to make thyself that which thou wishest to be, how canst thou expect to mold another in conformity to thy will? But we require perfection in the rest of mankind, and take no care to rectify the disorders of our own heart; we desire that the faults of others should be severely punished, and refuse the gentlest correction ourselves; we are offended at their licentiousness, and yet can not bear the least opposition to our own immoderate desires; we would subject all to the control of rigorous statutes and penal laws, but will not suffer any restraint upon our own actions. Thus it appears, how very seldom the second of the two great commandments of Christ is fulfilled, and how difficult it is for a man to "love his neighbor as he loves himself."

If all men were perfect, we should meet with nothing in the conduct of others to suffer for the sake of God. But in the present fallen state of human nature, it is his blessed will, that we should learn to "bear one another's burdens:" and as no man is free from some burden of sin or sorrow; as none has strength and wisdom sufficient for all the purposes of life and duty, the necessity of mutual forbearance, mutual consolation, mutual support, instruction, and advice, is founded upon our mutual imperfections, troubles, and wants. Besides, by outward occasions of suffering from the conduct of others, the nature and degree of every man's inward strength is more plainly discovered; for outward occasions do not make him frail, but only show him what he is in himself.

XVII. THE EXERCISES OF RELIGION.

---

30   If he be a member of the same individual church, the rule of further proceedings, if the offense be open, is found, Matt xviii., which every church member ought frequently to read.—Ed.

The life of a religious man ought not only so to abound with holiness, as that the frame of his spirit may be at least equal to his outward behavior; but there ought to be much more holiness within than is discernible without; because God, who searcheth the heart, is our inspector and judge, whom it is our duty infinitely to reverence. We ought every day to renew our holy resolutions, and excite ourselves to more animated fervor, as if it were the first day of our conversion; and to say: "Assist me, O Lord God, in my resolution to devote myself to thy holy service; and grant that this day I may begin to walk perfectly, because all that I have done hitherto is nothing."

According to the strength of our resolution, so is the degree of our progress; and much diligence and ardor is necessary for him who wishes to advance well: for if he whose resolutions are strong, often fails, what will he do, whose resolutions are weak? We break our resolutions, indeed, from various causes, and in various ways; and a slight omission of religious exercises seldom happens without some injury to the spirit.

The good resolutions of the righteous depend not upon their own wisdom and ability, but upon the grace of God, in which they perpetually confide, whatever be their attempts; for they know, that "though the heart of man deviseth his way," yet the Lord ordereth the event; and that "it is not in man that walketh, to direct his steps."

If for some act of piety, or some purpose of advantage to thy brother, a customary exercise is sometimes omitted, it may afterward be easily resumed; but if it is lightly relinquished through carelessness or weariness of spirit, the omission becomes culpable, and will be found hurtful. After the best exertion of our endeavors, we shall still be apt to fail in many duties. Some determined resolution, however, must always be made, especially against those tempers and habits that are the chief impediments to our growth in grace.

The concerns of our outward state, as well as of our inward spirit, are to be examined and regulated; because both have a considerable influence in obstructing or advancing the spiritual life. If thou canst not continually recollect thyself, do it sometimes at least, and not less than twice every day, in the morning and in the evening. In the morning resolve; and, in the evening, examine what thou hast that day been in thought, word, and deed; for in all these, perhaps, thou hast often offended God and thy brother. Gird thy loins like a valiant man, and be continually watchful against the malicious stratagems of the devil. Bridle the appetite of gluttony, and thou wilt with less difficulty restrain all other inordinate desires of animal nature. Never suffer the invaluable moments of thy life to steal by unimproved, and leave thee in idleness and vacancy; but be always either reading, or writing, or praying, or meditating, or employed in some useful labor for the common good.

The same kind of exercise is not equally suited to the state and improvement of every spirit; but some are more useful and convenient to one than to another. Different exercises are also expedient for different times and seasons; and some are more salutary for the days of feasting, and some for the days of fasting: we stand in need of some in the seasons of temptation, and of others in the hours of internal peace and rest: some subjects of meditation are fitter for a time of sorrow, and others when we "rejoice in the Lord."

When we expect to receive the Lord's Supper, or are about to observe any other special season of devotion, self-examination is an exercise peculiarly important and timely. Indeed, we ought at all times so to prepare our spirits, and so regulate our actions, as if we were shortly to be admitted into "the joy of our Lord." If that blessed event is still deferred, let us humbly acknowledge that we are not yet sufficiently prepared for that great "glory which shall be revealed in us," in God's appointed time: and may a contrite sense of such an improper state, quicken us to more faithful vigilance, and a more holy preparation. "Blessed is that servant, whom his Lord, when he cometh, shall find watching. Verily I say unto you, that he will make him ruler over all that he hath."

XVIII. SOLITUDE AND SILENCE.

Appropriate a convenient part of time to retirement and self-converse, and frequently meditate on the wonderful love of God in the redemption of man. Reject all studies that are merely curious; and read what will penetrate the heart with holy compunction, rather than exercise the brain with useless speculations.

If thou canst refrain from unnecessary conversation and idle visits, and suppress the desire of "hearing and telling some new thing;" thou wilt find not only abundant leisure, but convenient opportunity, for holy and useful meditation. It is the declaration of Seneca, that "as often as he mingled in the company of men, he came out of it less a man than he went in." To the truth of this our own experience, after much free conversation, bears testimony; for it is much easier to be wholly silent, than not to exceed in word; it is much easier to keep concealed at home, than to preserve ourselves from sin abroad: he, therefore, that presseth forward to the perfection of the internal and spiritual life, must, with Jesus, as much as possible, "withdraw him self from the multitude."

No man can safely go abroad, that does not love to stay at home; no man can safely speak, that does not willingly hold his tongue; no man can safely govern, that would not cheerfully become subject; no man can safely command, that has not truly learned to obey; and no man can safely rejoice, but he that has the testimony of a good conscience.

The joy of the saints has always been full of the fear of God; nor were they less humble, and less watchful over themselves, because of the splendor of their holiness, and their extraordinary measures of grace. But the security of the wicked begins in pride and presumption, and ends in self-delusion. Whatever, therefore, are thy attainments in holiness, do not promise thyself a state of unchangeable elevation in the present life. Those whose character for virtue has stood high in the esteem of men, have been proportionably more exposed to the danger of a severer fall through self-confidence. Therefore, it is much safer for most men not to be wholly free from temptation, but rather to be often assaulted, lest they grow secure, lest they exalt themselves in the pride of human attainments, nay, lest they become wholly devoted to the honors, pleasures, and comforts of their earthly life.

O that man would less anxiously seek after transitory joy, would less busy himself with the trifling affairs of a perishing world; how pure a conscience might he maintain! O that he could divorce his spirit from all vain solicitude, and, devoting it to the contemplation of God and the truths of salvation, place all his confidence in the divine mercy. In what profound tranquility and peace would he possess his soul!

No man is worthy of heavenly consolation, unless he hath been diligently exercised in holy compunction. If thou desirest true compunction, enter into thy closet, and excluding the tumults of the world, according to the advice of the

Psalmist, "commune with thy heart, and be still," that thou mayest feel regret and horror for sin. Thou wilt find in the closet that which thou often losest abroad. The closet long continued in becomes delightful; but when seldom visited, it is beheld with reluctance, weariness, and disgust. If, in the beginning of thy conversion, thou canst keep close to it, and cultivate the advantages it is capable of yielding, it will be ever after desirable as a beloved friend, and become the seat of true consolation.

In solitude and silence the holy soul advances with speedy steps, and learns the hidden truths of the oracles of God. There she riseth to a more intimate union with her Creator, in proportion as she leaves the darkness, impurity, and tumult of the world. To him who withdraws himself from his friends and acquaintances to seek after God, will God draw near with his holy angels. It is better for a man to lie hid, and attend to the purification of his soul, than, neglecting that "one thing needful," to go abroad and work miracles. Our sensual appetites continually prompt us to range abroad in search of gratification; but when the hour of wandering is over, what do we bring home but remorse of conscience, and weariness and dissipation of spirit? A joyful going out is often succeeded by a sad return; and a merry evening brings a sorrowful morning. Thus carnal joy enters delightfully, but ere it departs bites and kills.

What canst thou see anywhere else which thou canst not see in thy chosen retirement? Behold the heavens, the earth, and all the elements! For out of these were all things made. What canst thou see there or anywhere that will "continue long under the sun?" Thou hopest, perhaps, to subdue desire by enjoyment; but thou wilt find it impossible for "the eye to be satisfied with seeing, or the ear filled with hearing." If all nature could pass in review before thee, what would it be but a vain vision?

Lift up thy eyes, then, to God in the highest heavens, and pray for the forgiveness of thy innumerable sins and negligences. Leave vain pleasures to the enjoyment of vain men, and mind only that which God hath required of thee for thine own eternal good. Make thy door fast behind thee; and invite Jesus, thy Beloved, to come unto thee, and enlighten thy darkness with His light. Abide faithfully with Him in this retirement, for thou canst not find so much peace in any other place.

XIX. COMPUNCTION OF HEART.

If thou wouldst make any progress in the Christian life, keep thyself continually in the fear of God. Love not licentious freedom, but restrain all thy senses within strict discipline, and guard thy spirit against intemperate mirth. Give up thy heart to compunction, and thou wilt soon feel enkindled in the fire of devotion.

Compunction opens a path to infinite good, which is instantly lost by dissipation and merriment. It is wonderful that any man should rejoice in this life who considers his state of banishment, and the multitude of dangers to which he is continually exposed; but through levity of heart, and the neglect of self-examination, we grow insensible of the disorders of our souls, and often vainly laugh, when in reason we ought to mourn. There is, however, no true liberty, nor any solid joy, but in the fear of God united with a pure conscience.

Blessed is the man who can throw off every impediment of trouble and dissipation, and recollect his spirit into union with holy compunction! Blessed is he that can renounce every enjoyment that may defile or burden his conscience! Strive manfully; one custom is subdued and extirpated by another. If thou canst divorce thyself from men and their concerns, they will soon divorce themselves from thee, and leave thee to do the work of thy own salvation in peace.

Perplex not thy spirit, therefore, with the business of others, nor involve thyself in the interests of the great. Keep thy eye continually upon thyself as its chief object. Grieve not that thou dost not enjoy the favor of men, but rather grieve that thou hast not walked with that holy vigilance and self-denial which becomes a true Christian and a devoted servant of God.

It is more safe and beneficial not to have many consolations in the present life, especially those that are carnal. That we are destitute, however, of spiritual and divine consolation, or but seldom enjoy its sweetness, is owing to ourselves, because we desire not compunction of heart, nor abandon those consolations that are external and vain. Acknowledge thyself not only unworthy of divine consolation, but worthy rather of much tribulation.

When a man feels true compunction, the pleasures and honors of the world become burdensome and bitter, and he finds more occasion for grief and tears than for hilarity and self-complacency: for whether he considers himself, or thinks of others, he knows that no man lives without much tribulation. The more he considers himself, the greater will be his sorrow; for the ground of true sorrow, is the multitude of our transgressions, and the strong possession that sin has in us; by which our faculties are so subdued, that we are scarcely ever able to contemplate the enjoyments of the heavenly state.

If we did more frequently think of the time of death, than of the length of life, we would undoubtedly exert more ardent resolution in resisting the power of sin: but because we suffer not these considerations to impress our hearts, but turn them off by yielding to the blandishments of sense, we remain, both to the evil of our fallen state, and the means of redemption from it, cold and insensible.

XX. THE CONSIDERATION OF HUMAN MISERY.

Wretched art thou, wherever thou art, and to whatever thou turnest, unless thou turnest to God. Why art thou troubled because the events of life have not corresponded with thy will and desire? Who is there that enjoyeth all things according to his own will? There is no human being without some share of distress and anguish. Whose condition, therefore, is the best? His, surely, who is ready to suffer any affliction for the sake of God.

Many weak and ignorant persons say, "Behold, how happy a state does that man enjoy! How rich, how great, how powerful and exalted!" But turn thy attention to the unfading glories and unperishing riches of eternity, and thou wilt perceive that all these temporal advantages are in themselves of no value; their acquisition and continuance are uncertain, and their enjoyment painful; for they are never possessed without solicitude and fear. The happiness of man, whose real wants are soon and easily supplied, "consisteth not in the abundance of the things which he possesseth."

The more spiritual a man desires to be, the more bitter does he find the present life; because he more sensibly feels in himself, and more clearly discerns in others, the depths of human corruption. To eat and drink, to wake and sleep, to labor and rest, and to be subject to all the other necessities of fallen nature, must needs be a life of affliction to the regenerate man, who longs "to be dissolved," and to be free from sin, and the occasions of sin.

Miserable, however, are all who have not this sense of the corruption and misery of their present life, and much more miserable those that are in love with it; for there are some whose attachment to it is so exceedingly strong, that though by their own labor and the bounty of others, they are scarcely supplied with common necessaries, yet if it was possible for them to live here for ages, they would not spend a single thought on the kingdom of God. O, infatuated and faithless hearts, that are so deeply sunk in earth, as to feel no desire for any enjoyments but those that are carnal! Wretched creatures! They will in the end bitterly experience, how vain and worthless that is on which they have "set their affections."

The hour of distress is the hour of victory. Thou must pass through fire and water, before thou canst come to refreshment and rest. Unless thou dost violence to thyself, thou wilt never subdue sin. While we carry about us this corruptible body, we can not be free from the assaults of sin, nor live without weariness and sorrow. We desire, indeed, to be at rest from all misery; but as, by sin, we lost our innocence, so, with our innocence, we lost our true happiness. It is, therefore, necessary to hold fast our patience, and wait the appointed time of God's mercy, till this iniquity, and the calamities of which it is the cause, "shall be overpast, and mortality be swallowed up of life."

How great is human frailty, forever prone to evil! Today we confess our sins, and tomorrow commit the same sins again: this hour we resolve to be vigilant, and the next, act as if we had never resolved. What reason, therefore, have such corrupt and unstable creatures to be continually humble, and to reject every vain opinion of their own strength and goodness!

That may be soon lost through negligence, which after much labor we have at length scarcely attained through grace: and what will become of us in the eve of life, if we grow cold and languid in the morning? Woe be to us, if we thus turn aside to repose and ease, as if all were peace and security; when as yet there does not appear a single footstep of true holiness in all our conduct!

We have still need, like young novitiates, of being again instructed, and, by severe discipline, formed to holiness; if peradventure any hope be left of future amendment, and a more sure advancement toward the perfection of the spiritual life.

XXI. THE MEDITATION OF DEATH.

The end of the present life will speedily come: consider, therefore, in what degree of preparation thou standest for that which will succeed. Today man is, and tomorrow he is not seen; and when he is once removed from the sight of others, he soon passeth from their remembrance. O the hardness and insensibility of the human heart, that thinks only on present concerns, and disregards the prospects of futurity! In every thought, and every action, thou shouldst govern and possess thy spirit as if thou wast to die today; and were thy conscience pure, thou wouldst not fear dissolution, however near. It is better to avoid sin, than to shun death. If thou art not prepared for that awful event today, how wilt thou be prepared t-morrow? Tomorrow is uncertain; and how knowest thou that tomorrow will be thine?

What availeth it to live long, when the improvement of life is so inconsiderable? Length of days, instead of making us better, often increaseth the weight of sin. Would to God that we could live well only for one day! Many reckon years from the time of their conversion; but the account of their attainments in holiness, is exceedingly small. Therefore, though death be terrible, yet a longer life may be dangerous. Blessed is the man who continually anticipates the hour of his death, and keeps himself in preparation for its approach!

If thou hast ever seen another die, let not the impression of that most inter-esting sight be effaced from thy heart; but remember, that through the same vale of darkness thou also must pass. When it is morning, think that thou mayst not live till the evening; and in the evening, presume not to promise thyself another morning. Be, therefore, always ready; and so live that death may not confound thee at its summons.

Ah, foolish man! why dost thou still flatter thyself with the expectation of a long life, when thou canst not be sure of a single day? How many unhappy souls, deluded by this hope, are in some unexpected moment separated from the body! How often dost thou hear, that one is slain, another is drowned, another by falling from a precipice has broken his neck, another is choked in eating, another has dropped down dead in the exercise of some favorite diversion. Thousands are daily perishing by fire, by sword, by plague, or by robbers! Thus is death common to every age; and man suddenly passeth away as a vision of the night.

Thou too mayst die suddenly and unexpectedly; "for in such an hour as ye think not, the son of man cometh." And when that last hour is come to thee, thou wilt begin to think differently of thy past life, and be inexpressibly grieved for thy remissness and inconsideration. How wise and happy is the man who continually endeavors to be as holy in the day of life, as he wishes to be found in the hour of death! A contempt of the world, an ardent desire of improvement in holiness, cheerful obedience, self-denial, and the patient enduring of affliction for the sake of Christ, will contribute to raise a pleasing confidence of dying well.

While the mind is invigorated by health of body, thou wilt be able to do much toward thy purification; but when it is oppressed and debilitated by sickness, I know not what thou canst do. Few spirits are made better by the pain and languor of sickness.

Let not the example of thy friends and relations, nor any confidence in the superiority of their wisdom, influence thee to defer the care of thy salvation to a future time; for all men, even thy friends and relations, will forget thee much sooner than thou supposest. It is better to "provide oil for thy lamp" now, before it is wanted, than to depend upon receiving it from others "when the bridegroom cometh:" for if thou art not careful of thyself now, who can be careful of thee hereafter, when time and opportunity are forever lost? This instant, now, is ex-ceedingly precious: Now is the "accepted time, now is the day of salvation." How deplorable is it, not to improve this invaluable moment, in which we may lay hold on eternal life! A time will come when thou shalt wish for one day, nay one hour, to repent in; and who can tell whether thou wilt be able to obtain it?

Awake, then, and behold from what inconceivable danger thou mayst now be delivered; from what horrible fear thou mayst now be rescued, only by "pass-ing the time of thy sojourning in holy fear," and in continual expectation of thy removal by death. Endeavor now to live in such a manner, that in that awful mo-ment thou mayst rejoice rather than fear. Learn now to die to the world, that thou mayst then begin to live with Christ. Learn now to despise created things, that being delivered from every incumbrance, thou mayst then freely rise to him. Now subdue thy earthly and corruptible body by penitence and self-denial, that then thou mayst enjoy the glorious hope of exchanging it for a spiritual and immortal body, in the resurrection of the just.

Who will remember thee after death, and whose prayer can then avail thee? Now, therefore, O thou that readest! Turn to God, and do whatever his Holy Spirit enables thee to perform; for thou knowest not the hour in which death will seize thee, nor canst thou conceive the consequences of its seizing thee unprepared. Now, while the time of gathering riches is in much mercy continued, lay up for thyself the substantial and unperishing treasures of heaven. Think of nothing so much as the business of thy redemption, and the improvement of thy state before God. Now "make to thyself friends" of the regenerate and glorified sons of God, that when thy present life "shall fail, they may receive thee into everlasting habitations."

Live in the world as a stranger and pilgrim; and, knowing that thou hast "here no continuing city," keep thy heart disengaged from earthly passions and pursuits, and lifted up to heaven in the patient "hope of a city that is to come, whose builder and maker is God." Thither let thy daily prayers, thy sighs, and tears, be directed; that after death thy spirit may be wafted to the Lord, and united to him forever. Amen.

XXII. THE LAST JUDGMENT AND THE PUNISHMENT OF SINNERS.

In all thy thoughts and desires, thy actions and pursuits, "have respect to the end;" and consider how thou wilt appear before that awful Judge, from whom nothing is hidden, who is not to be perverted by bribes, nor softened by excuses, but invariably judgeth righteous judgment. O most wretched and foolish sinner, thou who tremblest before the face of an angry man that is ignorant in all things! What wilt thou be able to answer unto God, who knoweth all thy sins, and searcheth the lowest depths of the evil that is in thee? Why lookest thou not forward, to prepare thyself for the day of his righteous judgments, in which one man cannot possibly be excused or defended by another, but everyone will have as much as he can answer, in answering for himself?

The patient man hath in this world a true and salubrious purgatory; who, when he is injured, is more grieved for the sin of the offender, than for the wrong that is done to himself; who can ardently pray for his enemies, and from his heart forgive their offenses; who feels no reluctance to ask forgiveness of others; who is sooner moved to compassion, than provoked to anger; who constantly denies his own will, and endeavors to bring the body into absolute and total subjection to the spirit. But through an inordinate love for the indulgences of corrupt flesh and blood, we deceive ourselves into total ignorance and negligence with respect to all the interests of our immortal spirits.

The more thou now indulgest thyself, and gratifiest the desires of the flesh, the more fuel dost thou heap up as food for that fire which is never quenched. The pains of that tremendous state will arise from the nature and degree of every man's sins. There the spiritual sluggard shall be incessantly urged with burning stings, and the glutton tortured with inconceivable hunger and thirst: there the luxurious and voluptuous shall be overwhelmed with waves of flaming pitch and horrid sulphur; the envious with the pain of disappointed malignity, shall howl like mad dogs: the proud shall be filled with shame, and the covetous straitened in inexpressible want. One hour of torment there will be more insupportable than a hundred years of the severest sufferings and self-denial in this life. There no respite of pain, no consolation of sorrow can be found; while here some intermission of labor, some comfort from holy friends, is not incompatible with the most rigorous devotion.

Be now, therefore, solicitous for thy redemption, and afflicted for the sins that oppose it, that in the day of judgment thou mayst stand securely among the blessed. Then shall he rise up in judgment, who now meekly submits to the judgment of others; then the humble and poor in spirit shall have great confidence, and the proud shall be encompassed with fear on every side. Then it will be evident to all, that he was wise in this world, who had learned to be despised as a fool for the love of Christ: the remembrance of tribulation patiently endured shall become sweet, and "all iniquity shall stop her mouth." Then every devout man shall rejoice, and every impious man shall mourn. Then shall the mortified and subdued flesh triumph over that which was pampered in ease and indulgence; the coarse garment shall shine, and the soft raiment lose its luster; and the homely cottage shall be more extolled than the gilded palace. Then simple obedience shall be more highly prized than refined subtlety, and a pure conscience more than learned philosophy; the contempt of riches shall be of more value than all the treasures of worldly men; and thou shalt have greater comfort from having prayed devoutly every day, than from having fared deliciously; and shalt more rejoice that thou hast kept silence long, than that thou hadst talked much. Then works of holiness shall avail thee more than the multitude of fine words: and a life of self-denial shall give thee more satisfaction than all earthly delights could bestow.

Learn, therefore, now to suffer under afflictions comparatively light, that thou mayst be delivered from sufferings so grievous. Here thou mayst first make trial how much there thou wilt be able to sustain; for if thou art able to bear but little now, how wilt thou then bear such amazing and lasting torments? If only a slight suffering makes thee so impatient now, what will the rage of hell do then? Behold and consider! thou canst not have a double paradise; thou canst not enjoy a life of delight and pleasure upon earth, and afterward reign with Christ in Heaven.

If to this very day thou hadst lived in honor and pleasure, what would it avail if thou art to die the next moment? All, therefore, is vanity but the love of God, and a life devoted to His will. He that loveth God with all his heart, fears neither death, nor judgment, nor hell, because "perfect love casteth out fear," and openeth a sure and immediate access to the divine presence. But it is no wonder that he, who still loves and delights in sin, should fear both death and judgment. Yet, if thou art not to be withheld from sin by the love of God, at least be restrained from it by fear; for he that casts behind him the fear of an offended God, must run precipitately into every snare of the devil.

XXIII. ZEAL IN THE REFORMATION OF LIFE.

Be watchful and diligent in the service of God; and frequently recollect that thou hast left the broad way of the world, and entered into the narrow path of holiness, that thou mightest live to God, and become a spiritual man. With increasing ardor, "press" continually "toward the mark," and ere long thou wilt receive "the prize of the high calling of God in Christ Jesus;" when there shall be no more fear nor sorrow, for "God shall wipe all tears from our eyes," and take away all trouble from our hearts. Thus will a short life of inconsiderable labor be exchanged for an everlasting life, not only of perfect rest, but of increasing joy. If thou continue faithful and diligent in laboring, God doubtless will be faithful and rich in recompensing. Maintain, therefore, a comfortable hope that in the end thou shalt inherit the crown of victory; only beware of security, lest it betray thee into sloth or presumption.

Suppose a person deeply perplexed about the state of his soul, continually fluctuating between hope and fear, and overwhelmed with grief, were to repeatedly utter this wish: "O that I certainly knew that I should be able to persevere!" He might be answered thus: "And what wouldst thou do if this certain knowledge were bestowed upon thee? Do now that which thou wouldst then do, and rest secure of thy perseverance." If, comforted and established by this answer, he should resign himself to the divine disposal, his perplexity and distress would soon be removed. Instead of indulging anxious inquiries into the future condition of our soul, we should apply ourselves wholly to know what was "the good and acceptable will of God," as the only principle and perfection of every good work. "Trust in the Lord, and do good," saith the royal prophet; "so shalt thou dwell in the land, and be fed" with the riches of His grace.

The principal obstacle to the reformation and improvement of life, is dread of the difficulty and labor of the contest. Only they make eminent advances in holiness who resolutely endeavor to conquer in those things that are most disagreeable and most opposite to their appetites and desires; and then chiefly does a man most advance to higher degrees of the grace of God, when he most overcomes himself, and most mortifies his own spirit.

But though all men have not the same degree of evil to overcome, yet a diligent Christian, zealous of good works, who has more and stronger passions to subdue, will be able to make a greater progress than he that is inwardly calm, and outwardly regular, but less fervent in the pursuit of holiness.

Two things are highly useful to perfect amendment: to withdraw from those sinful gratifications to which nature is most inclined, and to labor after that virtue in which we are most deficient. Be particularly careful also to avoid those tempers and actions that chiefly and most frequently displease thee in others. Wherever thou art, turn everything to an occasion of improvement: if thou behold or hear of good examples, let them kindle in thee an ardent desire of imitation; if thou seest anything blamable, beware of doing it thyself; or if thou hast done it, endeavor to amend it the sooner. As thy eye observeth, and thy judgment censureth others, so art thou observed and censured by them.

The zealous and watchful Christian bears patiently, and performs cheerfully, whatever is commanded: but he that is cold and negligent suffers tribulation upon tribulation, and of all men is most miserable; for he is destitute of inward and spiritual comfort, and to that which is outward and carnal he is forbidden to have recourse. He that obstinately throws off the restraints of Christ's easy yoke, is not only in danger of irrecoverable ruin, but will find himself deceived in the expectation of a life of relaxation and liberty; for restraint, opposition, and disgust, will perpetually arise wherever he turns the imaginations and desires of his heart.

Consider the spiritual life of the Apostles and first followers of Christ as the object of thy imitation, and doubt not but the mercy of God, to all that turn the desire of their heart to Him, will enable thee to follow it. In this path thou mayst go forward with increasing hope and strength; and in this path thou wilt approach Heaven with such speedy steps as soon to despise and forget all human strength, consolation, and dependence.

When a man is so far advanced in the Christian life as not to seek consolation from any created thing, then does he first begin perfectly to enjoy God; then, "in whatever state he is, he will therewith be content then, neither can prosperity exalt, nor adversity depress him; but his heart is wholly fixed and established in

God, who is his All in All; with respect to whom nothing perisheth, nothing dieth, but all things live to His glory, and are continually subservient to His blessed will.

Be always mindful of the great end of temporary nature; and remember that time once lost will never return. Without perpetual watchfulness and diligence, holiness can never be attained; for the moment thou beginnest to relax in these, thou wilt feel inward imbecility, disorder, and disquietude.

If thou press forward with unabated fervor, thou shalt find strength and peace; and, through the mercy of God, and the love of holiness which His grace hath inspired, wilt perceive "thy yoke" become daily "more easy, and thy burden more light." Reflect that it is only the fervent and diligent soul that is prepared for all duty and for all events; that it is greater toil to resist evil habits and violent passions than to sweat at the hardest labor; that he who is not careful to resist and subdue small sins will insensibly fall into greater, and that thou shalt always have joy in the evening if thou hast spent the day well. Watch over thyself, therefore, excite and admonish thyself, and whatever is done by others, do not neglect thyself. Thou wilt make advances in imitating the life of Christ in proportion to the violence with which thou deniest thyself Amen.

BOOK TWO.

INSTRUCTIONS FOR THE MORE INTIMATE ENJOYMENT OF THE SPIRITUAL LIFE.

XXIV. INTERNAL CONVERSATION.

"The kingdom of God is within you," saith our blessed Redeemer. Abandon, therefore, the cares and pleasures of this wretched world, and turn to the Lord with all thy heart, and thy soul shall find rest. If thou withdrawest thy attention from outward things, and keepest it fixed upon what passeth within thee, thou wilt soon perceive the "coming of the kingdom of God;" for "the kingdom of God is that peace and joy in the Holy Ghost," which cannot be received by sensual and worldly men. All the glory and beauty of Christ are manifested within, and there he delights to dwell; his visits there are frequent, his condescension amazing, his conversation sweet, his comforts refreshing, and the peace that he brings passeth all understanding.

O faithful soul, dispose thy heart for the reception of this Bridegroom, who will not fail to fulfill the promise which he hath made thee in these words: "If a man love me, he will keep my words: and my Father will love him; and we will come unto him, and make our abode with him." Give, therefore, free admission to Christ, and exclude all others as intruders. When thou possessest Christ, thou art rich, and canst want no other treasure: he will protect thee so powerfully, and provide for thee so liberally, that thou wilt no more have need to depend on the caprice of men. Men are changeable and evanescent as "the morning cloud:" but Christ abideth eternally, and in him the fountain of strength and peace will flow forever.

Thou must not place any confidence in frail and mortal men, however endeared by reciprocal affection or offices of kindness: nor art thou to be grieved, when, from some change in their temper, they become unfriendly and injurious; for men are inconstant as the wind, and he that is for thee today, may tomorrow be against thee. But place thy whole confidence in God, and let him be all thy fear, and all thy love: He will answer for thee against the great accuser, and do that which is most conducive to thy deliverance from evil.

Here thou hast "no continuing city and whatever be thy situation, thou art "a stranger and a pilgrim," and canst never obtain rest till thou art united to Christ. Why, then, dost thou stand gazing about the earth, when the earth is not the seat of thy repose? Thy proper dwelling-place is heaven; and earthly objects are only to be transiently viewed as thou travelest to it; they are all hurried away in the resistless current of time, and thy earthly life with them; beware, therefore, of adhering to them, lest thou be bound in their chains, and perish in their ruin. Let thy thoughts dwell with the Most High, and thy desire and prayer ascend without intermission to Christ.

Christ was rejected of men; and, in the extremity of distress, forsaken by his disciples and friends. He chose to suffer thus, and to be thus deserted and despised; and dost thou complain of injury and contempt from others? Christ had enemies and slanderers; wilt thou have all men to be thy friends and admirers? How can thy patience be crowned in heaven, if thou have no adversity to struggle with on earth? Canst thou be the friend and follower of Christ, and not the partaker of his sufferings! Thou must, therefore, suffer with Christ, and for his sake, if thou indeed desirest to reign with him. If thou hadst but once "known the fellowship of the sufferings of Jesus," and been sensible, though in a small degree, of the divine ardor of his love, thou wouldst be more indifferent about thy own personal share in the good and evil of the present life; and far from courting the favor and applause of men, wouldst rather rejoice to meet with their reproach and scorn, for the sake of Jesus. He that loves Jesus, who is the Truth, and is delivered from the slavery of inordinate desire, can always freely turn to God; and raising himself in spirit above himself, enjoy some portion of the blessed repose of heaven.

That man is truly wise, and taught not of men, but of God, who perceiveth and judgeth of things as they are in themselves, and not as they are distinguished by names and general estimation. He that has known the power of the spiritual life, and withdrawn his attention from the perishing interests of the world, is not dependent on time or place for the exercise of devotion. He can soon recollect himself, because he is never wholly engaged by sensible objects. His tranquillity is not interrupted by bodily labor or inevitable business, but with calmness he accommodates himself to events as they take place. He is not moved by the capricious humors and perverse behavior of men; and constant experience has convinced him, that the soul is no further obstructed and disturbed in its progress toward perfection, than as it is under the power and influence of the present life.

If the frame of thy spirit was in right order, and thou wert inwardly pure, all outward things would conduce to thy improvement in holiness, and work together for thy everlasting good: and because thou art disgusted by a thousand objects, and disturbed by a thousand events, it is evident that thou art not yet "crucified to the world, nor the world to thee." Nothing entangles and defiles the heart so much, as the inordinate love of creatures. If thou canst abandon the hope of consolation in the enjoyments of earthly and sensual life, thou wilt soon be able to contemplate the glory and blessedness of the heavenly state; and wilt frequently partake of that spiritual consolation, which the world can neither give nor take away.

XXV. SUBMISSION TO REPROOF AND SHAME.

Regard not much what man is for thee, or who against thee; but let it be thy principal concern that God may be with thee in every purpose and action of life. Keep thy conscience pure, and God will be thy continual defense; and him whom God defends the malice of man hath no power to hurt. If thou hast learned to suffer in silence and persevering patience, thou shalt certainly see the salvation of the Lord: He knows the most proper season for thy deliverance, and will administer the most effectual means to accomplish it; and to his blessed will thou shouldst always be perfectly resigned. It is the prerogative of God to give help under every trouble, and deliverance from all dishonor.

It is useful for preserving the humility of our spirit, that other men should know and reprove our manifold transgressions: and in cases of injury among brethren, the more humble the acknowledgment of the offense is, the more effectually will the offended person be appeased and reconciled.

The humble man God protects and delivers; the humble he loves and comforts; to the humble he condescends; on the humble he bestows more abundant measures of his grace, and after his humiliation exalts him to glory; to the humble he reveals the mysteries of redemption, and sweetly invites and powerfully draws him to himself. The humble man, though surrounded with the scorn and reproach of the world, is still in peace; for the stability of his peace resteth not upon the world, but upon God.

Do not think that thou hast made any progress toward perfection till thou feelest that thou art "less than the least of all" human beings.[31]

XXVI. PEACEFULNESS.

First have peace in thy own breast, then thou wilt be qualified to restore peace to others. Peacefulness is a more useful acquisition than learning. The wrathful and turbulent man, who is always ready to impute wrong, turns even good into evil; the peaceful man turns all things into good. He that is discontented and proud, is tormented with jealousy of every kind: he has no rest himself, and will allow none to others; he speaks what he ought to suppress, and suppresses what he ought to speak; he is watchful in observing the duty of others, and negligent with respect to his own. But let thy zeal be exercised in thy own reformation before it attempts

---

31   "Though you may know abundance of people to be guilty of some gross sins with which you cannot charge yourself yet you may justly condemn yourself as the greatest sinner that you know; and that for these following reasons:—

"First, Because you know more of the folly of your own heart than you do of other people's; and can charge yourself with various sins that you only know of yourself; and cannot be sure that other sinners are guilty of them. So that as you know more of the folly, the baseness, the pride, the deceitfulness, and negligence of your own heart than you do of any one's else, so you have just reason to consider yourself as the greatest sinner that you know, because you know more of the greatness of your own sins than you do of other people's.

"Secondly, The greatness of our guilt arises chiefly from the greatness of God's goodness toward us; from the particular graces and blessings, the favors, the lights, and instructions that we have received from him. Every sinner knows more of these aggravations of his own guilt than he does of other people's, and, consequently may justly look upon himself to be the greatest sinner that he knows. How good God has been to other sinners, what light and instruction he has vouchsafed to them, what blessings and graces they have received from him, how often he has touched their hearts with holy inspiration, you cannot tell. But all this you know of yourself; therefore, you know greater aggravations of your own guilt, and are able to charge yourself with greater ingratitude than you can charge upon other people. This is the reason why the greatest saints have in all ages condemned themselves as the greatest sinners.

"In order, therefore, to know your own guilt, you must consider your own particular circumstances; your health, your sickness, your youth or age, your particular calling, the happiness of your education, the degrees of light and instruction that you have received, the good men that you have conversed with, the admonitions that you have had, the good books that you have read, the numberless multitude of divine blessings, graces, and favors that you have received, the good motions of grace that you have resisted, the resolutions of amendment that you have often broken, and the checks of conscience that you have disregarded. Perhaps the person so odious in your eyes, would have been much better than you are, had he been altogether in your circumstances, and received all the same favors and graces from God that you have.

"This is a very humbling reflection, and very proper for those people to make, who measure their virtues by comparing the outward course of their lives with that of other people's."—*Law's Serious Call to a Devout and Holy Life.*

the reformation of thy neighbor.

Some are very skillful and ingenious in palliating and excusing their own evil actions, but cannot frame an apology for the actions of others, nor admit it when it is offered. If thou desirest to be borne with, bear with others. O consider at what a dreadful distance thou standest from that charity which "hopeth, believeth, and beareth all things;" and from that humility which, in a truly contrite heart, knows no indignation nor resentment against any being but itself.

It is so far from being difficult to live in peace with the gentle and the good, that it is highly grateful to all that are inclined to peace; for we naturally love those most whose sentiments and dispositions correspond most with our own. But to maintain peace with the churlish and perverse, the irregular and impatient, and those that most contradict and oppose our opinions and desires, is a heroic and glorious attainment. Some preserve the peace of their own breasts, and live in peace with all about them; and some, having no peace in themselves, are continually employed in disturbing the peace of others: they are the tormentors of their brethren, and still more the tormentors of their own hearts. There are also some who not only retain their own peace, but make it their business to restore peace to the contentious. After all, the most perfect peace to which we can attain in this miserable life consists rather in meek and patient suffering than in an exemption from adversity; and he that has learned most to suffer will certainly possess the greatest share of peace: he is the conqueror of himself, the lord of the world, the friend of Christ, and the heir of heaven!

XXVII. SIMPLICITY AND PURITY.

Simplicity and purity are the two wings with which man soars above earth and all temporary nature. Simplicity is in the intention: purity is in the affection: simplicity turns to God, purity enjoys him.

No good action will be difficult and painful, if thou art free from inordinate affection: and this internal freedom thou wilt enjoy, when it is the one simple intention of thy mind to obey the will of God, and do good to thy fellow-creatures.

If thy heart was rightly disposed, every creature would be a book of divine knowledge: a mirror of life, in which thou mightest contemplate the eternal power and beneficence of the Author of Life; for there is no creature, however small and abject, that is not a monument of the goodness of God. Such as is the frame of the spirit, such is its judgment of outward things. If thou hadst simplicity and purity, thou wouldst be able to comprehend things without error, and behold them without danger: the pure heart safely surveys not only heaven, but hell.

If there be joy in this world, who possesses it more than the pure in heart? And if there be tribulation and anguish, who suffers them more than the wounded spirit?

As iron cast into the fire is purified from its rust, and becomes bright as the fire itself; so the soul that in simplicity and purity adheres to God, is delivered from the corruption of animal nature, and changed into the "new man formed "after the image of him that created him."

Those who suffer the desire of perfection to grow cold and languid, are terrified at the most inconsiderable difficulties, and soon driven back to seek consolation in the enjoyments of sensual life. But those, in whom that desire is kept alive and invigorated by continual self-denial, and a steady perseverance in that narrow path in which Christ has called us to follow him, find every step they take more and more easy, and feel those labors light that were once thought insurmountable.

XXVIII. CONSIDERATION OF OURSELVES.

We ought to place but little confidence in ourselves, because the light we have is small. We are often insensible of our inward darkness; and are impelled by passion, which we mistake for zeal. We severely reprove little failings in our brethren, and pass over enormous sins in ourselves; we quickly feel, and perpetually brood over, the sufferings that are brought upon us by others, but have no thought of what others suffer from us. We should prefer to all other cares, the care of our own improvement; and if strictly watchful over our own conduct, will be silent about the conduct of others. But to the divine life of the spiritual man we will never attain, unless we can withdraw our attention from all persons, and the concerns of all, and fix it upon self.

Tell me, if thou canst, where thou hast been wandering, when thou art absent from thy own breast: and after thou hast run about, and taken a hasty view of the actions and affairs of men, what advantage bringest thou home to thy neglected and forsaken self? He that desires peace of heart, must cast irrelevant things behind him, and keep God and his own spirit in his view. As thy progress to perfection depends much upon thy freedom from the cares and pleasures of the world, it must be proportionably obstructed by whatever degree of value they have in thy affections. Abandon, therefore, all hope of consolation from created things, not only as vain but dangerous; and esteem nothing truly honorable, pleasing, great, and worthy the desire of an immortal spirit, but God, and that which immediately tends to the improvement of thy state in him. The soul that truly loves God, despises all that is inferior to him. It is God alone, the Infinite and Eternal, who filleth all things, that is the life, light, and peace, of all blessed spirits.

XXIX. THE JOY OF A GOOD CONSCIENCE.

The "rejoicing" of a good man is "the testimony of a good conscience." A pure conscience is the ground of perpetual exultation: it will support us under the severest trials, and enable us to rejoice in the depths of adversity: but an evil conscience, in every state of life, is full of disquietude and fear. Thou wilt enjoy tranquillity, if thy heart condemn thee not. Therefore do not hope to rejoice but when thou hast done well. The wicked cannot have true joy, nor taste of inward peace; for "there is no peace to the wicked," saith the Lord; "but they are like the troubled sea when it cannot rest, whose waters cast up mire and dirt." If they say, "We are in peace; no evil shall come upon us; and who will dare to hurt us?" believe them not; for the anger of the Lord will suddenly rise up within them; their boasting shall vanish like smoke, and the thoughts of their hearts shall perish.

To "glory in tribulation," is not difficult to him that glories "in the cross of our Lord Jesus Christ." That glory which is given and received among men comes with fear and envy, and vanishes in disappointment and regret. The glory of the just is proclaimed by the voice of conscience, and not by the mouth of men: their joy is from God, and in God; and their rejoicing is founded in truth. He that aspires after true and eternal glory, values not that which is temporal; and he that seeks after the glory of the earth, proves that he neither loves nor considers the eternal glory of heaven.

He only can have great tranquility, whose happiness depends not on the praise and dispraise of men. If thy conscience was pure, thou wouldst be contented in every condition, and undisturbed by the opinions and reports of men concerning thee; for their commendations can add nothing to thy holiness, nor their censures take anything from it: what thou art, thou art; nor can the praise of the whole world make thee greater in the sight of God. The more, therefore, the attention is fixed upon the true state of thy spirit, the less wilt thou regard what is said of thee in the world. Men look only on the face, but "God searcheth the heart;" men consider only the outward act, but God the principle from which it springs.

To think of having done well without self-esteem, is an evidence of true humility; as it is our evidence of great faith, to abandon the hope of consolation from created things. He that seeks not witness for himself among men, shows that he has committed his whole state to God, and has the witness in his own breast: for it is "not he who commendeth himself," nor he who is commended by others, that "is approved but him only, saith the blessed Paul, "whom God commendeth."

XXX. JESUS TO BE LOVED ABOVE ALL.

Blessed is he who knows what it is to love Jesus, and for his sake to despise himself. To preserve this love, we must relinquish the love of self and all creatures; for Jesus will be loved alone. The love of the creatures is deceitful and unstable; the love of Jesus is faithful and permanent. He that adheres to any creature, must fail when the creature fails; but he that adheres to Jesus, will be established with him forever. Cherish his love, who, though the heavens and the earth should be dissolved, will not forsake thee, nor suffer thee to perish. Thou must one day be separated from all it at thou seest and lovest among created things, whether thou wilt or not: living and dying, therefore, adhere to Jesus, and securely commit thyself to his faithful protection, who, when nature fails, is alone able to sustain thee.

Such is the purity of thy Beloved, that he will admit of no rival for thy love; but will himself have the sole possession of thy heart, and, like a king, reign there with sovereign authority, as on his proper throne. If thy heart was emptied of self-love, and of the love of creatures whom thou lovest only for thy own sake, Jesus would dwell with thee continually. But whatever love thou hast for men, of which Jesus is not the principle and end, and whatever be their returns of love to thee, thou wilt find both to be utterly vain and worthless. O place not thy confidence in man; lean not upon a hollow reed! for "all flesh is as grass, and all the glory of man as the flower of grass: the grass withereth, and the flower thereof falleth away."

Of men thou regardest only the outward appearance, and, therefore, art soon deceived; and while thou seekest relief and comfort from them, thou must meet with disappointment and distress. If in all things thou seekest Jesus, thou wilt surely find him in all; and if thou seekest thyself, thou wilt, indeed, find thyself, but to thy own destruction. He who in all things seeks not Jesus, involves himself in more evil than the world and all enemies could heap upon him.

XXXI. THE FRIENDSHIP OF JESUS.

When Jesus is present, all is well, and no labor seems difficult; but when he is absent, the least adversity is insupportable. When Jesus is silent, all comfort withers; but the moment he speaks again, the soul rises from her distress. Thus Mary rose hastily from the place where she sat weeping for the death of Lazarus, when Martha said to her, "The Master is come, and calleth for thee." Blessed is the hour when Jesus calls us from affliction and tears, to partake of the joys of his Spirit!

How great is the hardness of the heart, without Jesus! How great its vanity and folly, when it desireth any good beside him! Is not the loss of him greater than the loss of the world? For what can the world profit without Jesus? To be without Jesus, is to be in the depths of hell: to be with him, is to be in Paradise. While Jesus is with thee, no enemy hath power to hurt thee. He that finds Jesus, finds a treasure of infinite value, a good transcending all that can be called good; and he that loseth Jesus, loseth more than the whole world. That man only is poor in this world, who lives without Jesus; and that man only is rich, with whom Jesus delights to dwell.

It requires skill to converse with Jesus, and wisdom to know how to keep him; but not the skill of men, nor the wisdom of this world. Be humble and peaceful, and Jesus will come to thee; be devout and meek, and he will dwell with thee. Without a friend, life is unenjoyed; and unless Jesus he thy friend, infinitely loved and preferred above all others, life will be to thee a desolation. It is madness to confide and delight in any other: rather choose that the whole world should combine to oppose and injure thee, than that Jesus should be offended at thy preferring the world to him. Of all that are dear to thee, let Jesus be the peculiar and supreme object of thy love. Men, even those to whom thou art united by the ties of nature and the reciprocations of friendship, are to be loved only for the sake of Jesus; but Jesus is to be loved for himself. Jesus alone is to be loved without reserve, and without measure; because, of all that we can possibly love, he alone is infinite goodness and faithfulness. For his sake, and in the power of his love, enemies are to be dear to thee, as well as friends; and let it be thy continual prayer, even for thy enemies, that all men may be blest with the knowledge and love of him.

Desire not to be admired and praised for the goodness that is in thee, as if it was thy own; for the praise of being good is the prerogative of God: his goodness alone is absolute and underived. Thou art good only by the communication of that goodness which, from eternity to eternity, dwells essentially in him. Aspire after such inward purity and freedom, that no affection to any creature may have power to perplex and enslave thee: have a heart divested of all selfish affections and earthly desires, "stand still, and see the salvation of the Lord." Indeed, to this exalted state thou canst not arrive, without the prevention and attraction of his grace, which will bring thee into union with his blessed Spirit.

When the grace of God thus lives and reigns in the heart of man, he has power to "do all things:" but when its divine influence is suspended, he feels himself left in the poverty and weakness of fallen nature, exposed to the lash of every affliction.

XXXII. ABSENCE OF COMFORT.

It requires no considerable effort to despise human consolation, when we are possessed of divine: but it is transcendent greatness, to bear the want of both; and, without self-condolence, or the least retrospection on our own imaginary worth, patiently to suffer desolation of heart for the glory of God. What singular attainment is it, to be peaceful and devout, while "the light of God's countenance is lifted up upon thee?" That man cannot but find his journey easy and delightful, whom the grace of God sustains: so that he neither feels burden, nor meets with obstruction, but is supported by Omnipotence, and conducted by Truth.

We perpetually seek after consolation, from the dread of the want of it; and it is with difficulty that man is so far divested of self, as not to seek it in his earthly and selfish state. It requires long and severe conflicts, entirely to subdue the earthly and selfish nature, and turn all the desire of the soul to God. He that trusts to his own wisdom and strength, is easily seduced to seek repose in human consolation: but he that truly loves Christ, and depends only upon his redeeming power within him, as the principle of holiness and truth, turns not aside to such vain comforts, but rather exercises self-denial, and, for the sake of Christ, endures the most painful labors.

When God bestows upon thee the consolations of the Spirit, receive them with all thankfulness: but remember, they are his gift, not thy desert; and, instead of being elate, careless, and presuming, be more humble, more watchful and devout in all thy conduct. The hour of light and peace may soon give place to days of darkness and temptation. Such vicissitudes are not unexpected to those who are experienced in the divine life. When thou findest so sad a change in thy state do not immediately despair, but with humility search thy heart for the causes of thy trial, and with prayer wait earnestly on God who is infinite in goodness as well as power, and who is both able and willing to renew the bounties of his grace in more abundant measures. The royal prophet thus describes his own case: "When I was in prosperity," and my heart was filled with the treasures of grace, "I said, I shall never be moved." But these treasures being soon taken away, and feeling in himself the poverty of fallen nature, he adds, "Thou didst turn thy face from me, and I was troubled." Yet in this disconsolate state, he does not despair; but with more ardor, raises his desire and prayer to God: "Unto thee, O Lord, will I cry, and I will make my supplication unto my God." He then testifies, that his prayer is accepted, and his prosperous state restored; "The Lord hath heard me, and hath had mercy upon me; the Lord is become my helper." And to show how this mercy and help were manifested, he adds, "Thou hast turned my mourning into joy, and hast compassed me about with gladness."

In what can I hope, or where place my confidence, but in infinite goodness, and the life, light, and peace of the Divine Spirit? For whether the conversation of holy men, the endearing kindness of faithful friends, the melody of music in psalms and hymns, the entertainment of ingenious books, nay, the instructions of the oracles of God; whether any or all these advantages are present, what do they all avail, what joy can they dispense, when the Holy Spirit is withdrawn from my soul, and I am left to the poverty and wretchedness of my fallen self? In such a state, no remedy remains but meek and humble prayer, and the total surrender of my will to the blessed will of God. "To him that overcometh," saith He who is "the First and the Last," "will I give to eat of the tree of life, which is in the midst of the Paradise of God."

I wish for no consolation that robs me of compunction; nor aim at any contemplation that will exalt me into pride: for everything that is high, is not holy; nor every desire pure; nor everything that is sweet, good; nor everything that is dear to man, pleasing to God. But acceptable, beyond measure, is that grace by which I am made more humble, and more disposed to deny and renounce myself.

Why seek rest, when thou art born to labor? Dispose thyself for patience rather than for consolation; rather for bearing the cross than for receiving joy. Who among those that are devoted to the world would not gladly receive the joys and consolations of the Spirit, if they could be obtained without relinquishing the pursuits of honor, wealth, and pleasure? The joys and consolations of the Spirit transcend the delights of the world and the pleasures of sense, as far as heaven transcends the earth: these are either impure or vain; those alone are holy, substantial, delightful, the fruits of that new nature which is born of God. False freedom and self-confidence greatly oppose the heavenly visitation.

XXXIII. THANKFULNESS FOR THE GRACE OF GOD.

"Render unto God that which is God's," and take to thyself that which is properly thy own; give him the glory of all thy good, and leave for thyself only the shame and punishment of all thy evil.

God, who is infinite in goodness, manifests that goodness in bestowing the gift of his Holy Spirit; man, who is wholly evil, shows that evil in not rendering back the gift with the thankfulness and praise of dependent wretchedness. The influences of God's Spirit in large measures are poured only upon the truly thankful, and from the proud is taken away that which is given to the humble.

Set thyself in the lowest place, and the highest shall be given thee; for the more lofty the building is designed to be, the deeper must the foundations be laid. The greatest saints in the sight of God are the least in their own esteem; and the height of their glory is always in proportion to the depth of their humility. Those that are filled with true and heavenly glory have no place for the desire of that which is earthly and vain; being rooted and established in God, they cannot possibly be lifted up in self-exaltation. Whatever good they have, they acknowledge to be received; and ascribing the glory of it to the Supreme Author of good, they "seek not honor one of another, but the honor that cometh from God alone." That God may be glorified in himself, and in all his saints, is the prevailing desire of their hearts, and the principal end of all their actions.

Be thankful for what thou receivest, and thou wilt receive more. Let that which is thought the least of God's gifts, be unto thee even as the greatest; for the dignity of the Giver confers dignity on all his gifts; and none can be small that is bestowed by the Supreme God. Even chastisement from him is to be gratefully received; for whatever he permitteth to befall us, he permitteth it to promote the important business of our redemption.

XXXIV. THE SMALL NUMBER OF THOSE THAT LOVE THE CBOSS.

Jesus has many lovers of his heaven, but few bearers of his cross; many that desire to partake of his comforts, but few that are willing to share in his distress; many companions of his table, but few of his hours of abstinence. All are disposed to rejoice with Jesus, but few to suffer sorrow for his sake: many follow him to the breaking of bread, but few to the drinking of his bitter cup: many attend with reverence on the glory of his miracles, but few follow the ignominy of his cross. Many seem to love Jesus while they are free from adversity, and bless him while they receive his consolations: but their confidence and their devotion vanish when tribulation cometh, and they sink either into murmuring or despair.

But they who love Jesus for himself, and not for their own comfort, will bless him in the depths of distress. Nay, should he continue to withhold his consolations from them, they would still continue to praise him, still give him thanks. But do not they deserve the name of hirelings who are forever seeking after comfort? Do not all prove that they are lovers of themselves more than lovers of Christ who desire and think of nothing but the repose and pleasure of their own minds?

Where is the man that serveth God without the hope of reward? Where, indeed, is that true "poverty of spirit" to be found which is divested of all that is thought rich and valuable in the creatures and self? This is "a pearl of great price," that is worthy to be sought after to the utmost bounds of nature! Though a man give all his substance to feed the poor, it is nothing; though he mortify the desires of flesh and blood by severe penance, it is little; though he comprehend the vast extent of science, he is far behind. Though he hath the splendor of illustrious virtue, and the ardor of exalted devotion, still he will want much if he still wants this "one thing needful," this poverty of spirit, which, after abandoning the creatures about him, requires him to abandon himself; to go wholly out of himself; to retain no leaven of self-love and self-esteem; but when he hath finished his course of duty, to know and feel, with the same certainty that he feels the motion of his heart, that he himself hath done nothing.

Such a man will set no value upon those attainments which, under the power of self-love, he would highly esteem; but, in concurrence with the voice of Truth, "when he has done all that is commanded him," he will always freely pronounce himself "an unprofitable servant." This is that poverty and nakedness of spirit which can say with the Psalmist, "Lord, in myself, I am poor and desolate!" And yet there is none so rich, none so free, none so powerful, as he, who renouncing himself and all creatures, can remain in the most abject state of self-abasement.

XXXV. THE NECESSITY OF BEARING THE CROSS.

This saying seems hard to all: "Deny thyself, take up thy cross, and follow me." But as hard a saying will be heard, when the same divine voice shall pronounce, "Depart from me, ye cursed, into everlasting fire!" They, therefore, who can now attentively hear, and patiently follow the call to bear the cross, will not be terrified at the sentence of the final judgment. In that awful day, the banner of the cross will be displayed in heaven; and all who have conformed their lives to Christ crucified, will draw near to Christ the Judge, with holy confidence. Why, then, dost thou fear to take up the cross?

In the cross is life, health, protection from every enemy; from the cross are derived heavenly meekness, true fortitude, the joys of the Spirit, the conquest of self, the perfection of holiness. There is no redemption, no foundation for the hope of the divine life, but in the cross. Take up thy cross, therefore, and follow Jesus in the path that leads to everlasting peace. He hath gone before, bearing that cross upon which he died for thee, that thou mightst follow, patiently bearing thy own cross, and upon that die to thyself for him: and if we die with him, we shall also live with him: "If we are partakers of his sufferings, we shall be partakers also of his glory."

Though thou disposest all thy affairs according to thy own fancy, and conductest them by the dictates of thy own judgment, still thou wilt continually meet with some evil, which thou must necessarily bear, either with or against thy will; and, therefore, wilt continually find the cross. Thou wilt feel either pain of body, or distress and anguish of spirit. Sometimes thou wilt experience the absence of inward comfort; sometimes thy neighbor will put thy meekness and patience to the test; and, what is more than this, thou wilt sometimes feel a burden in thyself, which no human help can remove, no earthly comfort lighten; but bear it thou must, as long as it is the blessed will of God to continue it upon thee. It is the blessed will of God, in permitting the darkness of distress, that we should learn such profound humility and submission, as to resign our whole state, present and future, to his absolute disposal.

The cross is always ready, and waits for thee in every place; run where thou wilt, thou canst not avoid it. Turn which way thou wilt, either to the things above, or the things below; to that which is within or without thee; thou wilt in all, certainly find the cross: and if thou wouldst enjoy peace, and obtain the unfading crown of glory, it is necessary that in every place, and in all events, thou shouldst bear it willingly, and "in patience possess thy soul."

If thou bearest the cross willingly, it will soon bear thee, and lead thee beyond the reach of suffering, where "God shall take away all sorrow from thy heart." But if thou bearest it with reluctance, it will be a burden inexpressibly painful, which yet thou must still feel; and by every impatient effort to throw it from thee, thou wilt only render thyself less able to sustain its weight.

Why hopest thou to avoid that, from which no human being has been exempt? Who among the saints hath accomplished his pilgrimage in this world, without adversity and distress? Even our blessed Lord passed not one hour of his most holy life, without tasting "the bitter cup that was given him to drink:" and, of himself, he saith, that "it behooved him to suffer, and to rise from the dead, and so to enter into his glory." And why dost thou seek any other path to glory, but that, in which, bearing the cross, thou art called to follow "the Captain of thy salvation?" The life of Christ was a continual cross, an unbroken chain of sufferings: and desirest thou a perpetuity of repose and joy? Though, like St. Paul, thou wert "caught up to the third heaven," yet thou wouldst not he exempt from suffering: for of St. Paul himself, his Redeemer said, "I will show him how great things he must suffer for my name's sake." To suffer, therefore, is thy portion; and to suffer patiently and willingly, is the great testimony of love and allegiance to thy Lord.

The regenerate man, as he becomes more spiritualized, has a quicker discernment of the cross, wherever it meets him; and his sense of the evils of his exile, as the punishment of his fallen life, increases in proportion to his love of God, and desires of reunion with him. But this man, thus sensible of misery, derives hope even from his sufferings; for while he sustains them with meek and humble submission, their weight is continually diminishing; and what to carnal minds is the object of terror, is to him a pledge of heavenly comfort. He feels that the strength, the life, and peace, of the new man, rise from the troubles, the decay, and death of the old, and from his desire of. conformity to his crucified Saviour, as the only means of restoration to his first perfect state in God, he derives so much strength and comfort under the severest tribulations, that he wisheth not to live a moment without them. Of the truth of this, the blessed Paul is an illustrious instance; who says of himself, "I take pleasure in infirmities, in reproaches, in necessities, in persecutions, in distresses, for Christ's sake; for when I am weak, then am I strong."

It is not in man to love and to bear the cross; to resist the appetites of the body, and to bring them under absolute subjection to the Spirit; to shun honors; to receive affronts with meekness; to despise himself, and willingly be despised by others; to bear, with calm resignation, the loss of fortune, health, and friends; and to have no desire after the riches, the honors, and pleasures of the world. If thou dependest upon thy own will and strength to do and to suffer all this, thou wilt find thyself as unable to accomplish it, as to create another world; but if thou turnest to the divine power within thee, and trustest only to that as the doer and sufferer of all, the strength of Omnipotence will be imparted to thee, and the world and the flesh shall be put under thy feet: armed with this holy confidence, and defended by the cross of Christ, thou needest not fear the most malignant efforts of thy great adversary the devil.

Dispose thyself, therefore, like a true and faithful servant, to bear with fortitude the cross of thy blessed Lord. Prepare thy spirit to suffer patiently the innumerable inconveniences and troubles of this miserable life; for it is patient suffering alone, that can either disarm their power or heal the wounds they have made.

When thou hast obtained so true a conquest over self-love, that the love of Christ shall make tribulation not only tolerable because unavoidable but welcome because beneficial, all will be well with thee. But while every tribulation is painful and grievous, and it is the desire of thy soul to avoid it, thou canst not but be wretched, and what thou laborest to shun, will follow thee wherever thou goest.

Thy life must be a continual death to the appetites and passions of fallen nature; and be assured, the more perfectly thou diest to thyself, the more truly wilt thou live to God. No man is qualified to understand the stupendous truths of redemption, till he has subdued impatience and self-love, and is ready to suffer adversity for the sake of Christ. If the condition of thy present life was left to thy own choice, thou shouldst prefer suffering affliction for the sake of Christ, to the uninterrupted enjoyment of repose and comfort; for this will render thee conformable to Christ and all his saints. Indeed, the perfection of our state, depends more upon the patient suffering of long and severe distress, than upon continual consolation and ecstasy.

If any way, but bearing the cross and dying to his own will, could have redeemed man from that fallen life of self in flesh and blood, which is his alienation from, and enmity to God, Christ would have taught it in his word, and established it by his example. But of all that desire to follow him, he has required the bearing of the cross; and, without exception, has said to all, "If any man will come after me, let him deny himself, take up his cross, and follow me."

When, therefore, we have read all books, and examined all methods, to find out the path that will lead us to heaven, this conclusion only will remain, that "through much tribulation we must enter into the kingdom of God."

BOOK THREE.

DIVINE ILLUMINATION

XXXVI. BLESSEDNESS OF INTERNAL CONVERSATION WITH CHRIST.

DISCIPLE: I will hear what the Lord my God will say.

CHRIST: Blessed is the soul that listeneth to the voice of the Lord, and from his own lips heareth the words of consolation! Blessed are the ears that receive the soft whispers of the divine breath, and exclude the noise and tumult of the world! Blessed are the eyes shut to material objects, and open and fixed upon those that are spiritual! Blessed are they that examine the state of the internal man; and, by continual exercises of repentance and faith, prepare the mind for a more comprehensive knowledge of the truths of redemption! Blessed are all who delight in the service of God; and who, that they may live purely to him, disengage their hearts from the cares and pleasures of the world!

DISCIPLE: Consider these transcendent blessings, O my soul, and exclude the objects of sensual desire, that thou mayst be able to hear and understand the voice of the Lord thy God. Thy beloved speaketh again.

CHRIST: I am thy life, thy peace, and thy salvation: keep thyself united to me, and thou shalt find rest. Desire not the transitory enjoyments of earth, but seek after the eternal enjoyments prepared for thee in heaven: for what are those transitory enjoyments, but delusion and snares? And what can all creatures avail thee, when thou hast forsaken the Creator? Abandon, therefore, created things, that by a faithful and pure adherence, thou mayst be acceptable to him in whom thou hast thy being, and, in union with his Spirit, enjoy everlasting felicity.

XXXVII. COMMUNION WITH GOD.

DISCIPLE: "Speak, Lord, for thy servant heareth. I am thy servant; give me understanding, that I may know thy testimonies." Incline my heart to the words of thy mouth: "Let thy speech distill as the dew!"

The children of Israel once said to Moses, "Speak thou with us, and we will hear: let not God speak with us, lest we die." I pray not in this manner: no, Lord, I pray not so; but, with the prophet Samuel, humbly and ardently entreat, "Speak, Lord, for thy servant heareth." Let not Moses speak to me, nor any of the prophets; but speak thou, O Lord God, the inspirer and enlightener of all the prophets: for thou alone, without their intervention, canst perfectly instruct me; but, without thee, they can profit me nothing.

Thy ministers can pronounce the words, but cannot impart the Spirit; they may entertain the fancy with the charms of eloquence; but if thou art silent, they do not inflame the heart. They administer the letter, but thou openest the sense;

they utter the mystery, but thou revealest its meaning; they publish thy laws, but thou conferrest the power of obedience; they point out the way to life, but thou bestowest strength to walk in it: "they water, but thou givest the increase;" their voice soundeth in the ear, but it is thou that givest understanding to the heart. Therefore, do thou, O Lord my God, Eternal Truth! Speak to my soul; lest, being outwardly warned, but not inwardly quickened, I die, and be found unfruitful: lest the word heard and not obeyed, known and not loved, professed and not kept, turn to my condemnation. "Speak," therefore, "Lord, for thy servant heareth:" "Thou" only "hast the words of eternal life!" O speak, to the comfort of my soul, to the renovation of my nature, and to the eternal praise and glory of thy own holy name!

CHRIST: Son, hear my words: words full of heavenly sweetness, infinitely transcending the learning and eloquence of all the philosophers and wise men of this world. "The words that I speak, they are spirit, and they are life;" not to be weighed in the balance of human understanding, nor perverted to the indulgence of vain curiosity; but to be heard in silence, and received with meek simplicity and ardent affection.

DISCIPLE: "Blessed is the man whom thou instructest, O Lord, and teachest him out of thy law; that thou mayst give him rest from the days of adversity," lest he be left desolate upon the earth.

CHRIST: I taught the prophets from the beginning, and till now cease not to speak; but many are deaf to my voice. Most men listen more attentively to the world than to God; they more readily submit to the painful tyranny of sensual appetites than to the mild and sanctifying restraints of God's holy will. The world promises only transitory joy, and men engage with ardor in its unholy service; I promise that which is supreme and everlasting, and their hearts are insensible and unmoved. Where is the man that serves and obeys me with that affection and solicitude with which the world and the rulers of it are served and obeyed? Even the sea exclaimeth, "Be thou ashamed, O Zion!" because, for a trifling acquisition of wealth or honor, a tedious and fatiguing journey is cheerfully undertaken; but, to obtain eternal life, not a foot is lifted from the earth. The sordid gain of perishing riches engages the pursuit and employs the industry of all; the most inconsiderable share of this imaginary property is obstinately and bitterly contested. For the vain expectation of a vainer possession, men dread not the fatigue of sleepless nights and restless days: but, deplorable insensibility! for unchangeable good, for an inestimable recompense, for unsullied glory and endless happiness, the least solicitude and the least labor is thought too dear a purchase.

Be ashamed, therefore, O slothful and discontented servant that the children of the world should with more ardor seek after destruction and death than thou dost eternal life; that they should rejoice more in vanity than thou in the truth. Their hope is, indeed, vain, as that on which it is erected; but the hope that dependeth on my promises is never sent empty away: what I have promised I will give, what I have said I will fulfill. "I am the rewarder of them that diligently seek me: I am he which searcheth" and trieth "the hearts" of the devout.

Write my words upon thy heart: ponder them day and night; in the time of trouble, thou wilt find their truth and efficacy: and what thou now readest and understandest not the day of temptation will explain. I visit man, both by trials and comforts; and continually read him two lessons, one to rebuke his selfishness and impurity, and the other to excite him to the pursuit of holiness. He that hath my word, and despiseth it, hath that which "shall judge him in the last day."

XXXVIII. INSTRUCTION HOW TO WALK BEFORE GOD.

DISCIPLE: O Lord my God, thou art my supreme and consummate good! What am I, that I should presume to open my lips before thee? I am thy least and most unprofitable servant; an abject worm; much more poor and contemptible than I am able to conceive! Yet remember me, O Lord, and have mercy upon me; for, without thee, I have nothing, can do nothing, and am nothing. Thou alone art just, and holy, and good; thy power is infinite, and the manifestations of it boundless. Remember, O Lord, the love that brought me into being; and as thou madest all things for the communication of thy perfections and blessedness, O fill me with thyself!

How can I sustain the darkness and misery of this fallen life, unless thy truth enlighten, and thy strength support me? O turn not away thy face, delay not thy fatherly visitation, suspend not the consolation of thy spirit, lest my soul become like a barren and "thirsty land where no water is!" Lord, "teach me to do thy will;" teach me to walk before thee in humility and faith, in fear and love! Thou art my wisdom, who knowest me in truth, and didst know me before I was born into the world, and before the world was made!

CHRIST: Son, walk before me in truth, and in singleness of heart seek me continually. He that walketh before me in truth, shall be defended against the assaults of evil spirits, and delivered from the delusions and calumnies of wicked men. "If the truth make thee free, thou shalt be free indeed;" and shalt hear, without emotion, the commendations or censures of the world.

DISCIPLE: Lord, thy word is truth! As thou hast spoken, so I beseech thee, be it done unto thy servant. Let thy truth teach, protect, and preserve me to my final redemption; let it deliver me from every evil temper and inordinate desire, so shall I walk before thee in "the glorious liberty of the children of God!"

CHRIST: I will teach thee what is my "good and acceptable and perfect will." Think on the evil that is in thee with deep compunction and self-abhorrence; and think on the good without self-esteem and self-exaltation. In thyself thou art a wretched sinner, bound with the complicated chain of many sensual and malignant passions. Thou art always tending to nothing and vanity; thou soon waverest, art soon subdued, soon disturbed, and easily seduced from the path of holiness and peace. There is in thee no good, which thou canst glory in as thy own; but much evil, requiring deep shame and self-abhorrence. Thou art even more dark, corrupt, and powerless, than thou art able to comprehend.

Let not pride deceive thee into false notions of the holiness and perfection of thy life; for thou hast nothing great, nothing valuable, nothing worthy of admiration and praise, nothing exalted, good, and desirable, but that which is produced by the operation of my Spirit. Let eternal truth be all thy comfort and thy boast, and thy own sinfulness thy displeasure and thy shame. Fear, abhor, and shun nothing so much as the evil tempers of thy fallen nature, and the evil habits of thy fallen life. These should offend and grieve thee more than all the losses and distresses we meet with in the world.

Some men walk not before me in simplicity and purity of heart; but moved by that curiosity and arrogance which deprived angels of heaven, and Adam of paradise, neglect themselves and their own salvation, to search into the counsels of infinite wisdom, and fathom the deep things of God. These fall into dangerous errors, and aggravated sins; and their pride and presumption I continually resist. But do thou fear the judgments of God, tremble at the wrath of Omnipotence; and, instead of questioning the proceedings of the Most High, search the depths of thy own iniquities, that thou mayst know how much evil thou hast done, and how much good thou hast neglected.

Some place their religion in books, some in images, and some in the pomp and splendor of external worship: these honor "me with their lips, but their heart is far from me." But there are some who, with illuminated understandings, discern the glory which man has lost, and with pure affections pant for its recovery. These hear and speak with reluctance of the cares and pleasures of the present life, and even lament the necessity of administering to the wants of animal nature. These hear and understand what the Holy Spirit speaketh in their heart, exhorting them to withdraw their affection from things on earth, and "set it on things above;" to abandon this fallen world, and day and night aspire after reunion with God.

XXXIX. THE POWER OF DIVINE LOVE.

DISCIPLE: I bless thee, O heavenly Father, the Father of my Lord Jesus Christ, that thou hast vouchsafed to remember so poor and helpless a creature! O Father of mercies, and God of all consolation, I give thee most humble and ardent thanks, that, unworthy as I am of all comfort, thou hast been pleased to visit my benighted soul with the enlivening beams of heavenly light! Blessing, and praise, and glory, be unto thee, and thy only-begotten Son, and the Holy Spirit, the Comforter, forever and ever!

O Lord my God, who hast mercifully numbered me among the objects of thy redeeming love, thou art my glory and my joy, my hope and refuge in the day of my distress. But my love is yet feeble, and my holy resolutions imperfect: do thou, therefore, visit me continually, and instruct me out of thy law; deliver me from malignant passions and sensual desires, that being healed and purified, I may love with more ardor, suffer with more patience, and persevere with more constancy.

CHRIST: Love is, indeed, a transcendent excellence, an essential and sovereign good; it makes the heavy burden light, and the rugged path smooth; it bears all things without feeling their weight, and from every adversity takes away the sting.

Divine love is noble and generous, prompting to difficult attempts, and kindling desire for greater perfection: it continually looks up to heaven and pants after its original and native freedom; and, lest its intellectual eye should be darkened by earthly objects, and its will captivated by earthly good, or subdued by earthly evil, sighs for deliverance from this fallen world.

Love surpasseth all sweetness, strength, height, depth, and breadth; nothing is more pleasing, nothing more full, nothing more excellent in heaven or in earth; for "Love is born of God;" and it cannot find rest in created things, but resteth only in him from whom it is derived.

Love is rapid in its motion as the bolt of heaven; it acts with ardor, alacrity, and freedom, and no created power is able to obstruct its course. It giveth all for all, and possesseth all in all; for it possesseth the Supreme Good, from whom, as from its fountain, all good eternally proceeds. It respecteth no gifts, but transcending all imparted excellence, turneth wholly to the Giver of every perfect gift.

Love knows no limits, feels no burden, considers no labor: it desires to do no more than, in its present state, it finds itself able to effect; yet it is never restrained by apparent impossibility, but conceives that all things are possible, and that all are lawful; it, therefore, attempts every labor, however difficult, and accomplishes many, under which the soul that loves not, faints and falls prostrate.

Love is watchful, and though it slumbereth, doth not sleep; it is often fatigued, but never exhausted; straitened, but not enslaved; alarmed by danger, but not confounded; and, like a vigorous and active flame, ever bursting upward, securely passeth through all opposition.

He that loveth, feels the force of this exclamation: "My God! my Love! Thou art wholly mine, and I am wholly thine!" and when this is the voice of love, it reacheth unto heaven.

DISCIPLE: Expand my heart with love, that I may feel its transforming power, and may even be dissolved in its holy fire! Let me be possessed by thy love, and ravished from myself! Let the lover's song be mine, "I will follow my beloved on high!" Let my soul rejoice exceedingly, and lose itself in thy praise! Let me love thee more than myself; let me love myself only for thy sake; and in thee love all others, as that perfect law requireth, which is a ray of the infinite love that shines in thee!

CHRIST: Love delights in the communication of good; and, with a swiftness equal to thought, diffuses its blessings with impartiality and ardor. It is courageous and patient, faithful and prudent, long-suffering and generous.

Love is circumspect, humble, and equitable; not soft, effeminate, sickly and vain, but sober, chaste, constant, persevering, peaceful and free from the influence of sensible objects. It is submissive and obedient to all, mean and contemptible in its own esteem, devout and thankful to God, and resigned even when his consolations are suspended, being faithfully dependent upon his mercy; for, in this fallen life, love is not exempt from pain.

He, therefore, that is not prepared to suffer all things, and, renouncing his own will, to adhere invariably to the will of his beloved, is unworthy of the name of lover. It is essential to that exalted character, to endure the severest labors and the bitterest afflictions, and to let nothing in created nature turn him aside from the supreme and infinite good.

XL. OF THE TRIAL OF TRUE LOVE.

CHRIST: Thou art yet far distant, my son, from the fortitude and purity of love; for thou art always seeking consolation with avidity; and the least opposition to thy inordinate desires, hath power to make thee relinquish thy most holy purposes. But he that has the fortitude of love, stands firm in the midst of temptations: and utterly disbelieves and despises the flattering insinuations of the enemy; he knows that I love him; and, whether in prosperity or adversity, makes me his supreme delight And he that loves with purity, considers not the gift of the lover, but the love of the giver; he values the affection more than the tokens of it; esteems his beloved infinitely beyond the benefits he confers; and, with a noble generosity divesting his mind of all desire of personal advantage, reposes himself not upon my gifts, but upon me.

Think not that all is lost, when thy heart is not elevated with that sensible fervor which thou art always coveting. These raptures are allowed thee as sweet foretastes of heavenly bliss, but thou art yet too carnal to be capable of their constant enjoyment. Seek then growth in grace, rather than flights of ecstasy. Thy principal concern and business is, to struggle against the motions of fallen nature, and the suggestions of fallen spirits; and if thou dost this with faithful perseverance, thou wilt give true proof of that Christian fortitude which will be distinguished by the crown of victory.

Let not strange temptations, that possess thee against thy will, disturb the quiet of thy soul. Maintain only an unchangeable resolution of obedience, and an upright intention toward God, and all will be well. Consider not thyself abandoned to the illusions of evil spirits, when, being suddenly elevated into holy ecstasy, thou as suddenly fallest into thy accustomed insensibility and dissipation of mind: if this change thou rather sufferest, than contributest to produce. While it is involuntary, and thou strivest against it, instead of being a proof of the loss of grace, it may be made an occasion of humble and acceptable resignation.

Know, that it is the continual labor of thy inveterate enemy, to suppress every holy desire in thy soul, and divert thee from every holy exercise; from affectionate meditation on my sufferings, from the imitation of my life, and the persevering constancy of the saints, from the profitable recollection of thy numerous sins, from the watchful keeping of thy own heart, and from the heaven-born resolution of "pressing toward the mark, for the prize of thy high calling." He disturbs thy thoughts by innumerable vain and sensual images, to create in thee disgust and abhorrence of the restraints of holiness, and to withdraw thee from prayer and the instructions of the oracles of God: he is offended and alarmed at an humble and contrite acknowledgment of sin; and, if possible, would bring thee to a total disuse of the memorials of my death. Believe him not, nor heed his power, though, to ensnare thy soul, he thus continually spreads his deceitful net. When he suggests vain thoughts, and impure desires, charge all the guilt upon his own head; and say to him, "Get thee behind me, unclean and malignant spirit! Depart from me, most detestable seducer! Thou shalt have no part in me: for Jesus, the bruiser of thy head, is with me; and like a mighty warrior, he will protect me from thy malevolence; and thou shalt fall subdued and confounded before him. I would rather die in extremity of torment, than consent to thy impious will. Hold thy peace, therefore, and be dumb forever: for I will hearken to thee no longer, nor have converse with thee, though thou shouldst continually invent new stratagems to rob me of holiness and peace." "The Lord is my light, and my salvation; of whom shall I be afraid? Though a host should encamp against me, my heart shall not fear. The Lord is my strength, and my Redeemer!" Thus, like a valiant soldier, let nothing abate thy struggle for victory; and if thou sometimes fallest, through human frailty, return to the mercy-seat with redoubled vigor, depending upon the abundant succors of my grace. Only beware of pride and self-complacency: for by these many are betrayed into error, till they are brought to a degree of blindness that is almost incurable. Let the destruction of the proud, who vainly presume upon their own wisdom and strength, be to thee a perpetual admonition of the blessings of humility.

XLI. ENJOYMENT MUST BE POSSESSED WITH HUMILITY.

CHRIST: My son, when the fire of devotion burns in thy heart, let not the favor exalt thee into pride: boast not of it as a distinction due to thy merit; nor ponder it in thy own mind with self-approbation and complacence. Rather in a the knowledge and distrust of thy great weakness, be more fearful in consequence of the gift, as bestowed upon one that may make an unworthy use of it. That ardor is not to be relied on which may soon abate, and give place to coldness.

During the enjoyment of heavenly consolation, recollect how poor and miserable thou wert without it. The advancement of spiritual life depends not upon the enjoyment of consolation, but upon bearing the want of it with resignation, humility, and patience, so as not to relinquish prayer, or remit any of thy accustomed holy exercises. Thou must, with a willing mind, and the best exertion of thy ability, perform all thy duties, and not abandon the care of thy improvement upon pretense of present barrenness and disquietude. There are many who, when their state of grace does not correspond with their eager desires and boundless expectations, instantly fall either into impatience or sloth; but "the way of man is not in himself;" and it belongeth unto God to give comfort when he pleases, to whom he pleases, and in that degree which is most subservient to the designs of his wisdom and goodness.

Some inconsiderate persons, by an improper use of the grace of devotion, have destroyed all its salutary effects. With an intemperate zeal grounded upon it, they have laid claim to such perfection as it is impossible to attain in the present life; not considering their own littleness, but following the tumultuous fire of animal passions instead of the calm irradiations of divine truth. These, by presumption and arrogance, have lost the grace that was vouchsafed them; and, though they had exalted themselves "as the eagles, and set their nest among the stars," yet they have fallen back into the poverty and wretchedness of nature; that, being stripped of all vain dependence upon themselves, they might learn that the best efforts of human strength are ineffectual, and that none can soar to heaven except I support his flight, and bear him upon my own wings.

They that are inexperienced in the spiritual life will be soon deceived, and easily subdued, unless they relinquish the guidance of their own opinions, and hearken to the counsels of tried and successful wisdom; but they who are "wise in their own conceit," have seldom humility enough to submit to the direction of others. An understanding, therefore, that is able only to "receive" the truths of "the kingdom of God" with the meekness and simplicity of "a little child," is infinitely better than that which, arrogantly glorying in its extent, can comprehend the utmost circle of science: "Better is it to be of an humble spirit" with the ignorant, "than to divide the spoils" of learning "with the proud."

That man acts indiscreetly who gives himself up to the joy of present riches, forgetful of his former poverty, and divested of that chaste and holy fear of God which makes the heart tenderly apprehensive of losing the grace it has received. Nor has he attained the fortitude of true wisdom who, in the day of distress and sadness, suffers his mind to be subdued by despair, and deprived of that absolute confidence in me, which is my right, and his own best support: but those that are most elate and secure in time of peace, are most fearful and dejected in time of war.

Trials will contribute more to the perfection of thy spirit than the gratification of thy own will in the enjoyment of perpetual sunshine. The safety and blessedness of man's state in this life are not to be estimated by the number of his consolations, nor by his critical knowledge of Holy Scripture, nor his exaltation to dignity and power, but by his being grounded and established in humility, and filled with divine charity, and by seeking in all he doth the glory of God.

DISCIPLE: "Shall I take upon me to speak unto my Lord, who am but dust and ashes?" If I think too highly of myself, and arrogate any excellence, behold, thou standest in judgment against me, and my iniquities oppose my claim by such true and forcible testimony that I can neither contradict nor elude. I feel and acknowledge the darkness, impurity, and wretchedness of my fallen nature. When I am left to the disorderly workings of nature and self, behold, I am all weakness and misery! But when thy light breaketh upon my soul, my weakness is made strong, and my misery turned into joy. And transcendently wonderful it is that a creature, which, by its alienation from thee, is always within the central attraction of selfishness and sin, should be so enlightened, purified, and blessed by a participation of the divine life! But this astonishing change is the pure effect of thy infinite love, producing in me all holy desires, succoring me in all necessities, protecting me from imminent dangers, and delivering me from innumerable unknown evils.

By the love of myself, I lost myself: but in the love and pursuit of thee alone, I have both found thee, and found myself; and this love, the purer it hath been, the more truly hath it shown me my own nothingness: for thou, O most amiable Saviour, hast been merciful unto me, beyond all that I could either ask, or hope, or conceive.

Blessed be thy name, O God! that, unworthy as I am of the least of all thy mercies, thou continuest to heap such innumerable benefits upon me. But thy love embraceth all, perpetually imparting light and blessings even to the ungrateful, and those that are wandered far from thee. O turn us back to thee again, that we may be thankful, humble, and wholly devoted to thy will: for thou art our wisdom, our strength, our righteousness, our sanctification and redemption!

XLII. ALL THINGS ARE TO BE REFERRED TO GOD.

CHRIST: If thou wouldst be truly blessed, my son, make me the supreme and ultimate end of all thy thoughts and desires, thy actions and pursuits. This will spiritualize and purify thy affections, which by an evil tendency are too often perverted to thyself and the creatures that surround thee: but if thou seekest thyself in the complacential honors of assumed excellence, or in the enjoyment of any good which thou supposest inherent in the creatures, thou wilt only find, both in thyself and them, the imbecility and barrenness of fallen nature. Refer, therefore, all things to me, as the giver of "every perfect gift;" the supreme good, from whom all excellence in the creatures is derived, and to whom alone the praise of excellence is due.

From me, as from a living fountain, the little and the great, the rich and the poor, draw the water of life; and he that willingly and freely drinks it to my glory, shall receive grace for grace: but he that glories in anything distinct from me, or delights in any good not referred to me, but appropriated as his own, cannot be established in true peace, nor find rest and enlargement of heart; but must meet with obstruction, disappointment, and anguish, in every desire, and every pursuit. Do not, therefore, arrogate good to thyself, nor ascribe good to any other creature; but render all to me, thy God, without whom, not only man, but universal nature, is mere want and wretchedness. I, who have given all, demand it back in grateful acknowledgment, and require of every creature the tribute of humble thanksgiving, and continual praise. In the splendor of this truth, all vain-glory vanisheth, as darkness before the sun.

When divine light and love have taken possession of thy heart, it will no longer be the prey of envy, hatred, and partial affections; for by divine light and love, the darkness and selfishness of fallen nature are totally subdued, and all its faculties restored to their original perfection. If, therefore, thou art truly wise, thou wilt hope only in me, and rejoice only in me, as thy everlasting life and light, perfection and glory: for "there is but one that is good, that is God;" who is to be blessed and praised above all, and in all.

DISCIPLE: I will now speak again unto my Lord, and will not be silent; I will say to my King, and my God, who sitteth in the highest heaven, "O how great" and manifold are the treasures of "thy goodness, which thou hast laid up for them that fear thee!" But what art thou, O Lord, to those that love thee with all their heart? Truly, the exquisite delight derived from that privilege of pure contemplation with which thou hast invested them, surpasseth the power of every creature to express. How free, and how exalted above all blessing and praise, is that goodness which thou hast manifested toward thy poor servant; which not only called him into being, but, when he had wandered far from thee, by its redeeming virtue brought him back to thee again, and with the command to love thee, conferred the power to fulfill it! O source of everlasting love! What shall I say concerning thee! How can I forget thee, who hast condescended to remember me, pining away and perishing in the poverty of sinful nature, and to restore me to the divine life! Beyond all hope thou hast shown mercy to thy servant, and beyond all thought hast made him capable of thy friendship, and dignified and blessed him with it. Poor and impotent as I am in myself, what can I render thee for such distinguished grace? For it is not given unto all, to renounce this fallen state; and, in abstraction from the cares and pleasures of the world, to follow thee in "the narrow path that leadeth unto life."

But is it a foundation of boasting, thus to serve thee, whom all creatures are bound to serve? Instead, therefore, of considering this call from vanity and sin, with self-complacency and approbation, as a superior distinction from other men; I ought rather to be lost in admiration and praise of thy condescending goodness, which has received so poor and unworthy a creature into thy family, and exalted him to the fellowship of thy faithful and beloved servants.

Lord, all that I have, all the ability by which I am made capable of serving thee, is thine; and thou, therefore, rather servest me. Behold, the heavens and the earth, which are continually ready to execute thy will, are made subservient to the redemption of fallen man; and what is more, thy holy "angels are ordained ministering spirits, and sent forth to minister for them who shall be heirs of salvation!" and, what infinitely transcendeth all, thou, the God of angels, hast condescended to take upon thee "the form of a servant" to man, and hast promised to give him thyself.

What returns of love and duty can I make thee, for these innumerable and astonishing dignities and blessings? O that I were able to serve thee all the days of my life! That I were able to serve thee truly, though but for one day! Thou art everlastingly worthy of all service, all honor, and all praise! Thou art my gracious Lord; and I am thy poor vassal, under infinite obligations to serve thee with all my strength, and perpetually to celebrate thy glorious name. To do this, is the sole wish and desire of my heart; and whatever ability is wanting in me to accomplish it, do thou in much mercy supply!

What exalted honor, what unsullied glory, to be devoted to thy service, and, for thy sake, to despise this fallen life, and all that is at enmity against thee! What large measures of grace are poured upon those who voluntarily subject themselves to thy most holy laws! What ravishing consolation do they receive from thy Holy Spirit, who, for the love of thee, renounce the delights of the flesh! What divine freedom do they enjoy, who, for the glory of thy holy name, leave "the broad way" of the world "that leadeth to destruction; and entering in at "the strait gate," persevere in "the narrow path that leadeth unto life!"

O happy and honorable service that makes man truly free and truly holy! O blessed privilege of filial adoption that numbers him with the family of heaven, makes him equal to the angels, and renders him terrible to evil spirits, and delightful to all that are sanctified! O service forever to be desired and embraced; in which we can enjoy the supreme and everlasting good!

XLIII. THE GOVERNMENT OF THE HEART.

CHRIST: Son, there are many things in which thou art not yet sufficiently instructed.

DISCIPLE: Lord, show me what they are, and enable me to understand and do them.

CHRIST: Thy desires must be wholly referred to me; and, instead of loving thyself, and following thy own partial views, thou must love only my will, and in resignation and obedience be zealous to fulfill it.

When desire burns in thy heart, and urges thee on some pursuit, suspend its influence for awhile, and consider whether it is kindled by the love of my honor or thy own personal advantage. If I am the pure principle that gives it birth, thou mayst yield thyself to its impulse without fear; and, whatever I ordain, thou wilt enjoy the event in tranquility and peace: but if it be self-seeking, hidden under the disguise of zeal for me, behold, this will produce obstruction, disappointment, and distress. It is always necessary to resist the sensual appetite, and by steady opposition subdue its power; to regard not what the flesh likes or dislikes, but to labor to bring it, whether with or against its will, under subjection to the spirit. And it must be thus opposed, and thus compelled to absolute obedience, till it is ready to obey in all things; and has learned to be content in every condition, to accept of the most ordinary accommodations, and not to murmur at the greatest inconvenience.

DISCIPLE: O Lord my God, from thy instruction, and my own experience, I learn the absolute necessity of patience: for this fallen state is full of adversity; and whatever care I take to secure peace, my present life is a continual trouble and warfare.

CHBIST: This, my son, will be the invariable condition of man till every root of evil is taken from him. But peace, so far from being found in a state that is free from temptation, and undisturbed by adversity, is derived only from the exercise of much tribulation, and the trial of many sufferings. Thinkest thou that the men of this world are exempt from suffering, or have but an inconsiderable portion? Thou wilt not find it thus, though thou searchest among the most prosperous and the most luxurious. Wilt thou say, that in the free indulgence of their own will, and the enjoyment of perpetual delight, their hearts are insensible to sorrow? And how long dost thou think this uncontrolled licentiousness and this uninterrupted enjoyment of sensual pleasure will last? Behold the mighty, the wise, and the rich, shall vanish like the cloud driven by tempest, and there shall be no remembrance of their honors or delights! Even while they live, the enjoyment of what they have is embittered by the want of what they have not; is either made tasteless by satiety or disturbed by fear; and that from which they expected to derive pleasure becomes the source of pain.

O, how transient and false, how impure and disgraceful, are mere earth-born pleasures! Yet, wretched man, intoxicated by perpetual delights, and blinded by custom, is insensible of the poison he imbibes; and for the momentary delights of an animal and corruptible life incurs the danger of eternal death!

Do thou, therefore, my son, restrain the appetites of the flesh, and turn away from thy own will: "Delight thyself in the Lord, and he shall give thee the desires of thy heart." If thou wouldst truly delight in me, and be plentifully enriched with the joys of my Spirit, know that such blessedness depends upon the conquest of the world, and the renunciation of its sordid and transitory pleasures; and the more thou abandonest the desire of finite good, the more truly wilt thou enjoy that infinite good which dwells in me.

But to the enjoyment of infinite good, thou canst not attain at once, nor without patient perseverance and laborious conflict. Inveterate evil habits will produce an opposition which can only be overcome by habits of holiness. The flesh will murmur and rebel, and it is only by increasing fervor of spirit that it can be silenced and subdued. The old serpent will deceive and trouble thee, and tempt thee to revolt; but he must be put to flight by ardent prayer, and his future approaches opposed by earnest vigilance and continual employment in some holy exercise or innocent and useful labor.

XLIV. OBEDIENCE AND SELF-ABASEMENT.

CHRIST: He that doth not freely and voluntarily submit to that superiority, under which my providence has placed him, demonstrates, that the flesh is not yet overcome. If, therefore, my son, thou desirest to subdue thy own flesh, learn ready and cheerful submission to the will of thy superiors: for that outward enemy will be much sooner overcome, if the mind is kept under strict discipline, and not suffered to waste its strength in dissipation and indulgence. There is not a more violent or more dangerous enemy than thy fleshly nature, when it does not freely consent to the law of the Spirit: thou must, therefore, be established in true self-abasement, if thou wouldst prevail against flesh and blood.

It is the inordinate love thou still indulgest for thy fallen self, that makes thee abhor submission to the will of others. Is it a great thing for thee, who art dust and ashes, to submit to man for the love of God; when I, the Supreme and Almighty, who created all things, submitted to man, for the love of thee? I became the least and lowest of all, that human pride might be subdued by my humility. Learn, therefore, to obey, O dust! learn to humble thyself, thou that art but earth and clay, and to bow down beneath the feet of all men! Learn to break the perverse inclinations of thy own will, that with ready compliance thou mayst yield to all demands of obedience, by whomsoever made. With holy indignation against thyself, suppress every intumescence of pride, till it can no longer rise up within thee; and till thou art so little and worthless in thy own eyes, that men may walk over thee, and as the dust of which thou art made, trample thee under foot. What hast thou to complain of, who art vanity itself? What, O base and unworthy sinner, canst thou answer to those who reproach and condemn thee, thou who hast so often offended God, and incurred his terrible wrath? But thy life was precious in my sight, and my eye hath spared thee, that thou "mayst know my love, which passeth knowledge;" and in a perpetual sense of my mercy and thy own unworthiness, devote thyself to unfeigned humility, cheerful submission, and a patient bearing of the contempt of mankind.

DISCIPLE: I stand astonished, when I consider that the heavens are not clean in thy sight. If thou hast found folly and impurity in angels, and hast not spared even them, what will become of me? If the stars have "fallen from heaven; if Lucifer, son of the morning," hath not kept his place; shall I, that am but dust, dare to presume upon my own stability? Many whose holiness had raised them to exalted honor, have been degraded by sin to infamy; and those that have fed upon the bread of angels, I have seen delighted with the husks of swine.

There is no holiness, if thou, Lord, withdraw thy presence; no wisdom profiteth, if thy Spirit cease to direct, no strength availeth, without thy support; no chastity is safe, without thy protection; no watchfulness effectual, when thy holy vigilance is not our guard. No sooner are we left to ourselves, than the waves of corruption rush upon us, and we sink; but if thou reach forth thy omnipotent hand, we walk upon the sea. In our own nature we are unsettled as the sand upon the mountain; but in thee, we have the stability of the throne of heaven: we are cold and insensible as darkness and death; but are kindled into light and life by the fire of thy love.

How worthless and vain should I deem the good that appears to be mine! With what profound humility, O Lord, ought I to cast myself into the abyss of thy judgments, where I continually find myself to be nothing! O depth immense! Where, now, is the lurking-place of human glory; where the confidence of human virtue? In the awful deep of thy judgments which cover me, all self-confidence and self-glory are swallowed up forever!

Lord, what is all flesh in thy sight? Shall the clay glory against him that formed it? Can that heart be elated by the vain applause of men, that has felt the blessing of submission to the will of God? The whole world has not power to exalt that which truth has subjected to himself; nor can the united praise of every tongue move him, whose hope is established in thee: for those that utter praise, behold they also are nothing, like those that hear it! they shall both pass away and be lost, as the sound of their own words; but "the truth of the Lord endureth forever!"

XLV. RESIGNATION TO THE DIVINE WILL.

CHRIST: Let this, my son, be the language of all thy requests: "Lord, if it be pleasing to thee, may this be granted, or withheld. Lord, if this tend to thy honor, let it be done in thy name. If thou seest that this is expedient for me, and will promote my sanctification, then grant it me, and with it grace to use it to thy glory: but if thou knowest it will prove hurtful, and not conduce to the health of my soul, remove far from me my desire." For every desire that appears to man right and good, is not born from heaven; and it is difficult always to determine truly, whether desire is prompted by the good Spirit of God, or the evil spirit of the enemy, or thy own selfish spirit; so that many have found themselves involved in evil, by the suggestions of Satan, or the impulse of self-love, who thought themselves under the influence and conduct of the Spirit of God.

Whatever, therefore, presents itself to the mind as good, let it be desired and asked in the fear of God, and with profound humility; but especially, with a total resignation of thy own will, refer both the desire itself and the accomplishment of it to me, and say, "Lord, thou knowest what is best: let this or that be done, according to thy will. Give me what thou wilt; and in what measure, and at what time thou wilt. Do with me as thou knowest to be best, as most pleaseth thee, and will tend most to thy honor. Place me where thou wilt, and freely dispose of me in all things. Lo, I am in thy hands; lead and turn me whithersoever thou pleasest: I am thy servant, prepared for all submission and obedience. I desire not to live to myself, but to thee: O grant it may be truly and worthily!"

DISCIPLE: Send thy Spirit, most merciful Jesus, "from the throne of thy glory," that it may be "present with me, and labor with me," and illuminate, sanctify, and bless me forever! Enable me always to will and desire that which is most dear and acceptable to thee. Let thy will be wholly mine: let it reign so powerfully in me that it may not be possible for me to oppose it, nor to like or dislike anything but what is pleasing or displeasing in thy sight!

Enable me to die to the riches and honors, the cares and pleasures, of this fallen world; and in imitation of thee, and for thy sake, to love obscurity, and to bear contempt. But transcending all I can desire, grant that I may rest in thee, and in thy peace possess my soul! Thou art its true peace, thou art its only rest; for, without thee, it is all darkness, disorder, and disquietude. In this peace, O Lord, even in thee, the supreme and everlasting good, I will "sleep and take my rest."

XLVI. TRUE COMFORT TO BE FOUND ONLY IN GOD.

DISCIPLE: Whatever I can desire or conceive as essential to my peace cannot be the production of the world, and in this world let me not seek it. If all the good of the present life was within my reach, and I had both liberty and capacity for its enjoyment, I know that it is not only changeable and evanescent, but is bounded by the grave. Thy full consolation and perfect delight, therefore, O my soul, are to found only in God, the comfort of the poor, and the exaltation of the humble. Wait a little while, wait with patience for the accomplishment of the Divine promise, which cannot fail, and thou shalt enjoy the plenitude of good in heaven. By the pursuit of earthly and finite good, thou losest that which is celestial and infinite; use this world, therefore, as "a pilgrim and a stranger," and make only the next the object of desire.

It is impossible thou shouldst be satisfied with temporal good, because thou wert not formed for it; and though all that the creatures comprehend was in thy possession, thou wouldst be still unblessed. It is in the Creator, the supreme God alone that all blessedness consists; not such as is extolled and sought after by the foolish lovers of the world, hut such as the faithful Christian admires and sighs for; such as the pure in heart, whose "conversation is in heaven," are sometimes permitted to foretaste.

How vain and transient is all human comfort! How substantial and permanent that which is derived from the Spirit of Truth living and ruling in the soul! The regenerate man continually turneth to Jesus, the comforter within him, and saith, "Be present with me, Lord Jesus! In all places, and at all times." May I find consolation in being willing to bear the want of all human comfort. And if thy consolation also be withdrawn, let thy will and righteous probation of me, be to me as the highest comfort; for "thou wilt not always chide, neither wilt thou keep thine anger forever!"

CHRIST: Son, suffer me always to dispose of thee according to my will; for that which is most profitable and expedient for thee is known only to me. Thy thoughts are the thoughts of a man, and partial affections pervert thy judgment.

DISCIPLE: Lord, all thy words are truth! Thy care over me is infinitely greater than all the care I can take for myself. His dependence is utterly vain who casteth not all his care upon thee.

Bring my will, O Lord, into true and unalterable subjection to thine, and do with me what thou pleasest; for whatever is done by thee cannot but be good. If thou pourest thy light upon me, and turnest my night into day, blessed be thy name; and if thou leavest me in darkness, blessed also be thy name; if thou exaltest me with the consolations of thy Spirit, or humblest me under the afflictions of fallen nature, still may thy holy name be forever blessed!

CHRIST: Let this, O my son, be the prevailing temper of thy spirit, if thou wouldst live in union with me: thou must be as ready to suffer as to rejoice, as willing to be poor and needy as to be full and rich.

DISCIPLE: Lord, I will freely suffer for thy sake, whatever affliction thou permittest to come upon me: I will indifferently receive from thee sweet and bitter, joy and sorrow, good and evil. For all that befalleth me, I will thank the love that prompts the gift, and reverence the hand that confers it. Keep me only from sin, and I will fear neither death nor hell: cast me not off forever, nor blot my name out of the book of life, and no tribulation shall have power to hurt me.

XLVII. MISERIES OF THIS LIFE TO BE BORNE WITH PATIENCE.

CHRIST: I came down from heaven, my son, for thy salvation; and took upon me the miseries of thy sinful nature, not from constraint but love, that thou mightst learn patience, and bear, without murmuring, the evils of thy fallen state. From the hour of my birth in the flesh to the hour of my expiration on the cross, I found no intermission of sorrow: I felt the extreme want of the necessaries of life: I heard the continual murmurings of the world against me in silence, and bore with meekness its reproach and scorn: my benefits were treated with ingratitude, my miracles with blasphemy, and my heavenly doctrine with misrepresentation and reproof.

DISCIPLE: O Lord! since thou, in whom was no sin, hast, by a life of patience and obedience, fulfilled thy Father's will; it is meet that I, a most wretched sinner, should patiently fulfill thy will and bear the evils of my fallen state, till the purposes of thy redeeming love are accomplished.

Though the present life is in itself a grievous burden, yet, through the power of thy grace, and the influence of thy example, and that of the saints who have followed thy steps, it is made supportable even to the weak. It is also enriched with comforts that were not experienced under the law, when the gate of paradise was obscured with shadows, and so few desired to seek after the kingdom of God. Nor could even those whom thou hadst chosen to salvation, and numbered among the just, "enter into the holiest," till, by thy stupendous passion and bitter death, "a new and living way" was consecrated for them.

O what thankfulness and praise are we bound to render thee, who hast thus condescended to open, for every faithful soul, a good and sure way to thy eternal kingdom! Thy life, O Lord, is our true way; and in the exercise of that holy patience which thy Spirit inspires, we approach nearer to thee, who art our righteousness and crown of glory. If thou hadst not shown us the path to life, and led us on by the united aid of thy example and thy grace, who could have found it, or who would have desired or been able to walk in it? If, blessed as we are, not only with the splendor of thy miracles and precepts, but with the irradiations of thy own Spirit, we are still cold, and indisposed to follow thee, what should we have been, if left in the darkness of fallen nature?

CHRIST: What hast thou said, my son? In the contemplation of my passion, and of the sufferings of those who have "followed me in the regeneration," suppress thy complaints: "thou hast not yet resisted unto blood." What are thy labors compared with those saints who have been so powerfully tempted, so grievously afflicted, so variously tried and exercised? In the remembrance of theirs which were so heavy, thou shouldst forget thy own which are so light. That thou thinkest thy sufferings not light, is owing to the impatience of self-love: but whether they are light or heavy, endeavor to bear all with patient submission.

The more truly thou disposest thyself to suffer, the more wisely dost thou act, and the greater will be thy recompense. By fortitude and habitual suffering, the severest evils are disarmed of their sting. Say not, "I cannot brook this injury from such a man; and the injury itself is what I ought not to bear; for he has done me irreparable wrong, and reproached me for evil that never entered my thoughts. From any other person I could have borne it without emotion; and there are many things that it is fit I should suffer." These are foolish distinctions, founded only on the nature of the offense, and the relation of the person who commits it, but regard not the virtue of patience, nor by whom it will finally be crowned.

He is not patient, who will suffer but a certain degree of evil, and only from particular persons. The truly patient man considers not by whom his trials come, whether by his superior, his equal, or his inferior; whether by the good and holy, or by the impious and the wicked. But whatever be the adversity that befalls him, however often it is renewed, or by whomsoever it is administered, he receives all with thankfulness, as from the hand of God, and esteems it great gain. There is no suffering, be it ever so small, that is patiently endured for the sake of God, which will not be honored with his acceptance and blessing.

If therefore thou desirest to obtain victory, make ready for the battle. The crown of patience cannot be received where there has been no suffering. If thou refuse to suffer, thou refusest to be crowned; but if thou wish to be crowned, thou must fight manfully, and suffer patiently: without labor, none can obtain rest; and without contending, there can be no conquest.

DISCIPLE: O Lord! make that possible to me by grace, which I find impossible by nature. Thou knowest that I can bear but little, and by the lightest adversity am soon overwhelmed. Grant that every tribulation and chastisement may be welcome, yea, even desirable to me for thy name's sake!

XLVIII. CONFESSION OF PERSONAL INFIRMITIES.

DISCIPLE: I will "confess my transgressions unto the Lord," and acknowledge my infirmity. How small are the afflictions by which I am often cast down, and plunged in sorrow! I resolve to act with fortitude, but by the slightest evil am confounded and distressed. From the most inconsiderable events, the most grievous temptations rise against me; and while I think myself established in security and peace, the smallest blast, if it be sudden, hath power to bear me down.

Behold, therefore, O Lord! my abject state, and pity the infirmity which thou knowest infinitely better than myself! Have mercy upon me, that I sink not; that the deep may not swallow me up forever! So apt am I to fall, and so weak and irresolute in the resistance of my passions, that I am continually driven back in the path of life, and covered with confusion in thy sight. Though sin does not obtain the full consent of my will, yet the assaults of it are so frequent, and so violent, that I am often weary of living in perpetual conflict. My corruption and weakness are experimentally known: for the evil thoughts that rush upon me, take easy possession of my heart, but are with difficulty driven out again.

O that thou, the mighty God of Israel, the zealous lover of faithful souls, wouldst look down with compassion on the labors and sorrows of thy servant, and perfect and fulfill his desire of reunion with thee. Strengthen me with heavenly fortitude, lest the old man, this miserable flesh, which is not yet brought under subjection to the Spirit, should prevail and triumph over me: against him I am bound to struggle, as long as I breathe in this fallen life.

Alas! what is this life, which knows no intermission of distress and sorrow! Where snares are laid, and enemies rise, both behind and before, on the right hand and on the left! While one tribulation is departing, another cometh on; and before the adversary is withdrawn from one severe conflict, he suddenly sounds a new alarm! And can a life like this, thus embittered with distress, thus filled with corruption, and subject to such a variety of evils, be the object of desire? Can it even deserve the name of life, when it is continually teeming with plagues and pains that terminate in death? Yet it is still loved and desired; and many place their whole confidence in it, and seek their supreme happiness from it.

The world, indeed, is frequently reproached for its deceitfulness and vanity; but while carnal affections govern the heart, it is not easily forsaken. It is both loved and hated by those who have neither inclination nor power to leave it: "the lust of the flesh, the lust of the eye, and the pride of life," being the offspring of the world, love it as their parent; but as these bring forth pain and misery, they bring forth also, in union with them, disgust and hatred of the world. But alas! while the soul is devoted to the delights of sin, the love of the world still prevails; and because she is a stranger to the joys of the Spirit, and hath neither tasted nor conceived the transcendent sweetness of communion with God, she still adheres to the world, and notwithstanding her manifold disappointments, still hopes to find pleasures hidden under thorns.

Those only who live to God in the continual exercise of faith and love, of patience, humility, resignation, and obedience, obtain the conquest of the world; and enjoy those Divine comforts that are promised to every soul that forsakes all to follow Christ: and those only truly discern how grievously the lovers of the world are mistaken; and in how many various ways they are defrauded of happiness, and left destitute and wretched.

XLIX. THE SOUL SEEKING REPOSE IN GOD.

DISCIPLE: Thy repose, O my soul, is to be found only in the supreme God, the everlasting rest and blessedness of the saints!

O most lovely, and most loving Jesus grant me the will and power, above all created beings, to rest in thee: above all health and beauty, all glory and honor, all power and dignity, all knowledge and wisdom, all riches and all arts; above all promise and hope, all holy desires and actions, all gifts and graces which thou thyself canst bestow, all rapture and transport which the heart is able to receive: above angels and archangels, and all the hosts of heaven; above all that is visible and invisible; and finally above everything, which thou, my God, art not!

For thou, O Lord God, art above all, in all perfection! Thou art most high, most powerful, most sufficient, and most full! Thou art most sweet, and most abundantly comforting! Thou art most lovely, and most loving; most noble and most glorious! In thee all good centers, from eternity to eternity! Therefore, whatever thou bestowest on me, that is not thyself; whatever thou revealest or promisest, while I am not permitted truly to behold and enjoy thee, is insufficient to fill the boundless desires of my soul, which, stretching beyond all creatures, and even beyond all thy gifts, can only be satisfied in union with thy all-perfect Spirit.

Dearest Jesus, spouse of my soul, supreme source of light and love, and sovereign Lord of universal nature! O that I had the wings of true liberty, that I might take my flight to thee, and be at rest! When will it be granted me, in silent and peaceful abstraction from all created being, to "taste and see how good" thou art, O Lord, my God! When shall I be wholly absorbed in thy fullness! When shall I lose, in the love of thee, all perception of myself; and have no sense of any being but thine!

Now I groan continually, and bear with pain the burden of my wretchedness: for innumerable evils spring up in this vale of sin and sorrow, that darken, deceive, and distress my soul; so that I can have no free access to thee, nor enjoy that ineffable communion with thee, which is the privilege and perfection of beatified spirits. O let my sighs, and the multiplied desolation which I suffer, move thee.

Holy Jesus, ineffable splendor of eternal glory, sole comfort of the wandering soul, my heart is lifted up to thee, and without voice speaketh to thee in "groanings that cannot be uttered!" How long will my Lord delay his coming? O may he come to me, his forlorn creature, and turn my sorrow into joy! May he reach forth his Omnipotent hand, and bid the winds that howl about me, be silent; and the sea that threatens to devour me, be calm! "Come, O Lord Jesus, come quickly!" In thy absence, no day nor hour is joyful: for thou art my only joy; and without thee my table is empty. I am a wretched prisoner in the darkness of this fallen world, bound with the chains of sin and misery till thou revivest me with thy presence, restorest me to liberty, and liftest up the light of thy reconciled countenance upon me.

Those that prefer the enjoyments of the world before thee, seek that happiness which they can never find. I will pursue no good, present or future, but thee alone, my God, my hope, and everlasting salvation: nor will I cease from my importunity till thou turnest to me again, and I hear thy blessed voice speaking within me.

Lord, I have called upon thee in my distress, and desire truly to enjoy thee, for I am prepared to renounce all things for thy sake. It is thou who hast given me both the will and the power to seek after thee: and forever blessed be thy name, O Lord! who, in the multitude of thy tender mercies, hast shown this transcendent kindness!

What hath thy servant to say more in thy presence, but to beg, that he may humble himself exceedingly before thee, and be ever mindful of his own darkness, impurity, and malignity. There is none like unto thee in all the wonders of heaven and earth; and all that thou doest, is, like thyself, supremely good: thy judgments are true; and thy Providence governeth the whole universe, that it may finally partake of thy perfection and blessedness. Praise and glory, therefore, be unto thee, O wisdom of the Father, forever! "Bless the Lord, all his works, in all places of his dominion: bless the Lord, O my soul!"

L. THE DIVERSITY OF GIFTS.

DISCIPLE: Open my heart, O Lord, in thy law, and teach me to walk in thy commandments. Give me understanding to know thy will; and to remember, with faithful recollection and profound reverence, thy innumerable benefits, as well general as personal, that I may be always able worthily to praise thee, and give thee thanks. I know, and confess, that of myself I am not able to render thee due praise for thy smallest benefit: for I am less than the least of all thy mercies; and when I attempt to contemplate thine excellent majesty, my spirit fails, unable to sustain the vast idea.

All faculties of mind and body, all endowments of nature, and all advantages of grace, are the gifts of thy hand, and proclaim the infinite love and munificence of the Giver, from whom all good eternally proceeds: and though one receiveth more, and another less, yet it is all thine, and without thee the least portion cannot be enjoyed.

He that hath received great gifts hath no reason to glory, nor to exalt himself above others, nor to insult his brother who hath received less. He is the greatest and best who ascribes least to himself, and is most devout and humble in the acknowledgment and praise of that infinite liberality from which every good and perfect gift proceeds: he only who esteems himself vile, and most unworthy of receiving the least favor, is qualified to discern and bless the bounty which confers the greatest.

He that hath received sparingly, ought not, therefore, to be troubled, to murmur at, or envy the larger portion of his wealthy brother; but rather, in humble resignation to thy will, O God, extol that universal goodness, which is so abundantly, freely, voluntarily, and without respect of persons, dispensed to all. Thou art the inexhaustible fountain of good; and for all that flows from it, thou only art to be praised. Thou knowest what is fit to be given, and what to be withheld; and why one hath more, and another less, is not in us, but in thee only to discern, who hast weighed the ability and state of all creatures in thy righteous balance.

Therefore, O Lord God, I esteem it a signal mercy that I do not possess many of those qualities and endowments which in the eyes of men appear glorious, and attract admiration and applause. Did we truly consider the Divine economy of providence and grace, so far from being disquieted, grieved, and dejected, we should rather derive comfort from considering that God has chosen the poor in spirit, the humble, the self-despised, and the despised of the world, for intimate friends, and the children of his family. Of this, the apostles are eminent instances, who were appointed to "sit on twelve thrones, judging the twelve tribes of Israel." These passed a life of indignity and opposition without complaint, and even rejoiced to "suffer shame for the name of Jesus;" and with ardent affection embraced that poverty which the world despises, and with unshaken patience endured those afflictions which the world abhors.

Nothing, therefore, should give so much joy to the heart of him that truly loveth thee, O God, and is truly sensible of thy undeserved mercies, as the perfect accomplishment of thy blessed will, not only in his temporal, but in his eternal state. He should feel so much complacency and acquiescence as to be abased as willingly as others are exalted; to be as peaceful and contented in the lowest place as others are in the highest, and as gladly to accept of a state of weakness and meanness as others do of the most splendid honors and the most extensive power. The accomplishment of thy will, and the glory of thy name, should transcend all other considerations, and produce more comfort and peace than all the personal benefits which have been or can possibly be conferred.

LI. FOUR STEPS THAT LEAD TO PEACE.

CHRIST: I will now teach thee, my son, the way to peace, and to true liberty of spirit.

DISCIPLE: Gracious Lord! do what thou hast condescended to offer. Such instruction I shall rejoice to hear, for such I greatly need.

CHRIST: 1. Constantly endeavor to do the will of another, rather than thy own; 2. Constantly choose rather to want less, than to have more; 3. Constantly choose the lowest place, and to be humble to all; and 4. Constantly desire and pray, that the will of God may be perfectly accomplished in thee, and concerning thee.

Verily, I say unto thee, he that doeth this, enters into the region of rest and peace.

DISCIPLE: Lord! this short lesson teacheth great perfection; it is expressed in few words, but it is replete with truth and fruitfulness. If I could faithfully observe it, trouble would not so easily rise up within me; for as often as I find myself disquieted and oppressed, I know I have wandered from the strait path which thou hast now pointed out. But do thou, O Lord! who canst do all things, and evermore lovest the improvement of the soul, increase the power of thy grace, that I may be enabled to fulfill thy word, and accomplish the salvation to which thou hast mercifully called me.

"O God, be not far from me: O my God, make haste for my help;" for a multitude of evil thoughts have risen up within me, and terrible fears afflict my soul. How shall I pass them unhurt? How shall I break through them, and adhere to thee?

CHRIST: I will go before thee, and humble the lofty spirits that exercise dominion over thee: I will break the doors of thy dark prison, and reveal to thee the secrets of my law.

DISCIPLE: *Prayer against Evil Thoughts.* Do, O Lord! what thou hast graciously promised: lift up the light of thy countenance upon my soul, that every thought which is vain and evil may vanish before it. This is my strength and comfort, to fly to thee in every tribulation, to confide in thy support, to call upon thee from the lowest depths of my heart, and patiently to wait for the superior consolations of thy Spirit.

O most merciful Jesus! restrain my wandering thoughts that are carried out after evil, and repulse the temptations that so furiously assault me.

A Prayer for Divine Illumination. Fight thou my battles; and with thine Omnipotent arm scatter all my enemies, those deceitful lusts, and malignant passions, that are continually at work to betray and destroy me. In thy power may I obtain peace, that my purified soul, as a living temple consecrated to thee, may resound with songs of thankfulness and praise! Rebuke the storms that rise within me. Say to the sea, "Be still;" and to the north wind, "Blow not;" and a heavenly calm shall instantly succeed.

Send forth thy light and thy truth, that they may "move upon" this barren "earth:" I am as the "earth, without form, and void;" a deep covered with darkness, till thou sayest, "Let there be light." Pour forth thy treasures from the throne of grace; water my heart with the dew of heaven, that the barren soil may produce good fruit worthy to be offered up to thee. Raise my fallen soul, oppressed with the burden of sin; draw all my desire after thee; and give me such a perception of the permanent glories of heaven, that I may despise and forget the fleeting vanities of earth! O force me from myself! Snatch me away from the delusive enjoyment of creatures, who are unable to appease my restless desires! Unite me to thyself by the indissoluble bonds of love; for thou only canst satisfy the lover, to whom the whole universe, without thee, is "vanity and nothing!"

LII. INSPECTION INTO THE CONDUCT OF OTHERS.

CHRIST: Son, indulge not vain curiosity, nor surrender thy spirit to the dominion of unprofitable cares: "what is that to thee? follow thou me." What, indeed, to thee, are the words, the actions, and characters of the idle and the busy, the ignorant and the vain? The burden of thy own sins is as much as thou canst bear, thou wilt not be required to answer for the sins of others; why perplex thyself with their conduct? Behold, I understand the thoughts afar off, and nothing that is done under the sun can escape my notice. I search the personal secrets of every heart, and know what it thinks, what it desires, and to what its intention is principally directed. All inspection, therefore, and all judgment being referred to me, do thou study only to preserve thyself in true peace, and leave the restless to be as restless as they will. They cannot deceive Omniscience; and whatever evil they have done or said, it will fall upon their own heads.

Hunt not after that fleeting shadow, a great name; covet not a numerous acquaintance, nor court the favor and affection of particular persons; for these produce distraction and darkness of heart. I would freely visit thee with instruction, and reveal my secrets to thee, if, in abstraction from cares, thou didst faithfully watch my coming, and keep the door of thy heart open to receive me. Be wise: "watch and pray;" and humble thyself continually, under the sense of thy numerous imperfections and wants.

LIII. IN WHAT PEACE AND PERFECTION CONSIST.

CHRIST: Son, I once said to my disciples, "Peace I leave with you; my peace I give unto you; not as the world giveth, give I unto you." Peace is what all desire; but the things that belong to peace, few regard. My peace dwells only with the humble and the meek, and is found only in the exercise of much patience. If thou wilt hearken to me, and obey my voice, thou mayst enjoy a large portion of true peace.

DISCIPLE: Lord I what shall I do?

CHRIST: Keep a strict guard over all thy words and actions; let the bent of thy mind be to please me only, and to desire and seek after no good but me; and if, with this, thou refrainest from censuring the words and actions of other men, and dost not perplex thy spirit with business that is not committed to thy trust, thou wilt but seldom feel trouble, and never feel it much.

Indeed, to be wholly exempt from trouble, and suffer no distress either of mind or body, belongs not to thy present life, but is the prerogative of that perfect state where evil is not known. Think not, therefore, that thou hast found true peace, when thou happenest to feel no burden of sin or sorrow; that all is well, when thou meetest with no adversary; neither exalt thyself in thy own esteem because thou hast felt the raptures of devotion, and tasted the sweetness of spiritual fervor: for by these marks the lover of perfection is not known; nor doth perfection itself, and man's progress toward it, consist in such exemptions and enjoyments.

DISCIPLE: In what then, O Lord?

CHRIST: In offering up himself with his whole heart, to the will of God; never seeking his own will either in small or great respects, either in time or in eternity;

but with an equal mind, weighing all events in the balance of the sanctuary, and receiving both prosperity and adversity with continual thanksgiving.

If, when deprived of spiritual comfort, thou prepare thy heart for severer trials, not justifying thyself, and extolling thy holiness as that which ought to have exempted thee from such sufferings, but justifying me in all my appointments; then thou wilt walk in the direct path to true peace, and thy spirit will be supported with the sure hope of seeing my face again in unutterable joy. The ground of this high attainment is an absolute contempt and forgetfulness of self; and when that is established, know that thou wilt enjoy peace in as full abundance as it can possibly be enjoyed in this state of exile from heaven!

DISCIPLE: Lord! it is the prerogative of a regenerate man never to relax in his desire after his first state in thee; and in the midst of innumerable cares and dangers that surround him, to pass on without solicitude, not from insensibility, but by a power of liberty peculiar to the mind that is delivered from inordinate affection to the creatures. I beseech thee, therefore, O my most merciful God, to preserve me from the cares of this fallen life, that my thoughts may not be darkened and perplexed; from the importunate wants and necessities of the body, that I may not be ensnared by the love of sensual pleasure; and from all impediments to the regenerate life, that I may not be subdued and cast down by trouble and despair.

O my God! who art benignity and sweetness inexpressible! Turn into bitterness all such consolation, as draws my mind from the desire of eternity. O my God! let not flesh and blood subdue me; let not the world, and the transient glory of it, deceive me; let not the devil, and his subtle reasoning, supplant me. Give me courage to resist, patience to suffer, and constancy to persevere! Give me, instead of worldly comfort, the divine unction of thy Holy Spirit; and for carnal love, pour into my heart the love of thy blessed name!

Behold, the care of food and raiment, which it is difficult to separate from vain decoration, and the indulgence of the sensual appetite, is grievous and burdensome to a fervent spirit. Grant me grace, therefore, to use all things pertaining to the body with moderation, and not anxiously to desire the possession of them, nor bitterly lament the want. To cast all away, the law of nature does not permit; for nature must be sustained: but to desire superfluity, and that which ministers to delight more than to use, the holy law forbids, lest the flesh should grow insolent, and rebel against the Spirit In all these difficult and dangerous paths, let thy wisdom and power govern and direct me, that I may not deviate to the right hand nor to the left.

LIV. SELF-LOVE THE CHIEF OBSTRUCTION TO THE ATTAINMENT OF THE SUPREME GOOD.

CHRIST: My son, thou must give all for all, and make an absolute surrender of thyself to me. The inordinate love of self is more hurtful to the soul than the united power of the world: for the creatures of the world have no dominion over thee but in proportion to the affection and desire with which thou adherest to them for thy own sake. If thy love was pure and fixed only upon me, no creature would have power to enslave thee. Covet not that which thou art not permitted to enjoy; retain not the possession of that which will obstruct thee in the pursuit of true good, and rob thee of inward liberty. How can it be that from the depth of thy heart thou dost not resign thyself, and all thou canst desire and possess, to my will!

Why dost thou pine away in useless sorrow? Why is thy strength consumed by superfluous cares? Establish thyself in absolute resignation to my good pleasure, and thou canst suffer no evil. But if, for thy own appropriate good, and the gratification of thy own will, thou desirest change of enjoyment, and seekest change of place, thou wilt always be tormented with anxiety, and made more restless by disappointment; for in all earthly good thou wilt find a mixture of evil to embitter its possession, and in every place meet some adversary to oppose thy will. It is not the acquisition nor the increase of external good, that will give thee repose and peace; but rather the contempt of it, and rooting the very desire out of thy heart: not only of the luxury of wealth, but of the pomp of glory, and the enjoyment of praise.

Neither can change of place avail, if there is wanting that fervent spirit devoted to me, which makes all places alike. Peace sought for abroad, cannot be found; and it will never be found by the heart, that, while it is destitute of me, wants the very foundation upon which alone peace can be established. Thou mayst change thy situation, but canst not mend it: the evils which thou hast fled from will still be found, and more may soon arise; for thou hast taken with thee the fruitful root of every evil, thy own unsubdued selfish will.

DISCIPLE: "Uphold me, O God, with thy free Spirit! Strengthen me with might in the inner man!" that being emptied of all selfish solicitude, I may no longer be the slave of restless and tormenting desires; but with holy indifference may consider all earthly good, of whatever kind, as continually passing away, and my own fallen life as passing with it: for there is nothing permanent under the sun, where "all is vanity and vexation of spirit."

But what wisdom, O Lord, can consider this truly, but that which was present with thee when thou madest the world, and knew what was acceptable in thy sight? O send me this wisdom "from the throne of thy glory," that I may learn to know and seek thee alone, and thus seeking find thee. May I love thee, and delight in thee, above all beings; may I understand all that thou hast made as it is in itself, and regard its various forms only according to that order in which thy infinite mind hath disposed them!

Grant that I may carefully shun flattery, and patiently bear contradiction; that being neither disturbed by the rude breath of impotent rage, nor captivated by the softness of delusive praise, I may securely pass on in the path of life, which, by thy grace, I have begun to tread.

LV. THE CRUEL CENSURES OF MEN NOT TO BE REGARDED.

CHRIST: Be not impatient, my son, when men think evil of thee, and speak that which thou art not willing to hear. Thy own opinion of thyself should be much lower than others can form, because thou art conscious of imperfections which they cannot know. If thy attention and care were confined to the life of the internal man, thou wouldst not feel the influence of fleeting words that dissolve in air. In times of ignorance and wickedness like this, it is most wise to bear reproach in silence, and in full conversion of thy heart to me not to regard the judgment of men.

Let not thy peace then depend upon the commendation or censure of ignorant and fallible creatures like thyself, for they can make no alteration in thy real character. True peace and true glory are to be found only in me; and he that seeking them in me loves not the praise of men, nor fears their blame, shall enjoy peace in great abundance. By love of human praise, and fear of human censure, nothing but disorder and disquietude are produced.

LVI. SUBMISSION TO GOD IN THE HOUR OF TRIBULATION.

DISCIPLE: Blessed be thy name, O Lord, forever, who hast permitted this tribulation to come upon me! I am not able to fly from it; but it is necessary for me to fly to thee, that thou mayst support me under it, and make it instrumental to my good. I am in deep distress, and my heart faints and sinks under the burden of its sorrows. Dearest Father, encompassed thus with danger, and oppressed with fear, what shall I say?—O save me from this hour!—But for this cause came I unto this hour, that, after being perfectly humbled, thou mightst have the glory of my deliverance. Be pleased, O Lord, to deliver me! Poor and helpless as I am, what can I do, and whither shall I go, without thee? O fortify me under this new distress; be thou my strength and my support; and whatever be its weight, whatever its continuance, I will not fear.

Lord, thy will be done! This tribulation and anguish I accept as my due: O that I may bear it with patience till the dark storm be overpast, and light and peace succeed! Yet thy omnipotent arm, O God, my mercy, as it hath often done before, can remove even this trial from me, or so graciously mitigate its severity that I shall not utterly sink under it. Though difficult it seems to me, how easy to thee is this change of thy right hand, O Most High!

CHRIST: "I am the Lord, a stronghold in the day of trouble;" when, therefore, trouble rises up within thee, take sanctuary in me. The support of heavenly consolation comes slowly, because thou art slow in the use of prayer; and before thou turnest the desire and dependence of thy soul to me, hast recourse to other comfort, seeking from the world or within thyself that relief which neither can bestow. Thy own experience should convince thee, that no profitable counsel, no effectual help, no lasting remedy, is to be found, but in me. When, therefore, I have calmed the violence of the tempest, and restored thy fainting spirit, rise with new strength and confidence in the light of my mercy; for I, the Lord, declare, that I am always near, to redeem all fallen nature from its evil, and to restore it to its first state, with superabundant communications of life, light, and love.

Dost thou think, that "there is anything too hard for me?" or that I am like vain man, who promiseth and performeth not? Where, then, and what is thy faith? O believe, and persevere! Possess thy soul in patience, and comfort will arrive in its proper season. Wait for me; and, if I come not, wait; for I will at length come, and "will not tarry." That which afflicts thee, is a trial for thy good; and that which terrifies thee is a false and groundless fear. What other effect doth thy extreme anxiety about the events of to-morrow produce, than the accumulation of anguish upon anguish? Remember my words, "Sufficient unto the day is the evil thereof." It is unprofitable and vain to be dejected or elevated by the anticipation of that which may never come to pass. Such disorders of imagination are, indeed, incident to fallen man; but it is an evidence of a mind that has yet recovered little strength, to be so easily led away by every suggestion of the enemy; who cares not, whether it is by realities or fictions, that he tempts and betrays thee: whether it is by love of present good, or the fear of future evil, that he destroys thy soul.

"Let not thy heart be troubled," neither let it be afraid. "Believe in me," whose redeeming power has "overcome the world," and place all thy confidence in my mercy. I am often nearest thee, when thou thinkest me at the greatest distance; and when thou hast given up all as lost in darkness, the light of peace is ready to break upon thee. All is not lost, when thy situation happens to be contrary to thy own narrow and selfish judgment. It is injurious to thy peace, to determine what will be thy future condition, by arguing from present perceptions; and it is sinful to suffer thy spirit to be so overwhelmed by trouble, as if all hopes of emerging from it were utterly taken away.

Think not thyself condemned to total dereliction, when I permit tribulation to come upon thee for a season, or suspend the consolations which thou art always fondly desiring; for this is the narrow way to the kingdom of heaven: and it is more expedient for my servants to be exercised with many sufferings, than to enjoy that perpetual rest and delight which they would choose for themselves. I, who know the hidden thoughts of thy heart, and the depth of the evil that is in it, know, that thy salvation depends upon thy being sometimes left in the full perception of thy own impotence and wretchedness; lest, in the undisturbed prosperity of the spiritual life, thou shouldst exalt thyself for what is not thy own, and take complacence in vain conceit of perfection, to which man of himself cannot attain.

The good I bestow, I can both take away and restore again. When I have bestowed it, it is still mine; and when I resume it, I take not away that which is thine; for there is no good of which I am not the principle and center. When, therefore, I visit thee with adversity, murmur not, neither let thy heart be troubled; for I can soon restore thee to light and peace, and change thy heaviness into joy; but in all my dispensations, acknowledge, that I, the Lord, am righteous, and greatly to be praised. If thou wert wise, and didst behold thyself and thy fallen state, by that light with which I, who am the Truth, enlighten thee; instead of grieving and murmuring at the adversities which befall thee, thou wouldst rejoice and give thanks: nay, thou wouldst "count it all joy, thus to endure chastening." I once said to the disciples whom I chose to attend my ministry upon earth, "As the Father hath loved me, so have I loved you;" and I sent them forth into the world, not to luxury, but to conflict; not to honor, but to contempt; not to amusement, but to labor; not to take repose, but to "bring forth much fruit with patience." My son, remember my words!

LVII. CREATOR TO BE FOUND IN ABSTRACTION FROM CREATURES.

DISCIPLE: O my God, what grace do I still want, to be able continually to turn to thee without adherence to the creatures; who, while they retain the least possession of my heart, keep me at a tremendous distance from thee! He truly desired this liberty, who said, "O that I had wings like a dove I for then would I fly away, and be at rest." And what can be more at rest, than the heart that in singleness and simplicity, regardeth only thee? What more free than the soul that hath no earthly desires? To be able, therefore, in peaceful vacancy, and with all the energy of my mind, to contemplate thee, and know that thou infinitely transcendest the most perfect of thy works, it is necessary that I should rise above all created beings, and utterly forsake myself; for, while I am bound with the chains of earthly and selfish affections, I find it impossible to adhere to thee.

CHRIST: Few, my son, attain to the blessed privilege of contemplating the infinite and unchangeable good, because few totally abandon that which is finite and perishing. For this, a high degree of grace is necessary, such as will raise the soul from its fallen life, and transport it above itself. And unless man, by this elevation of spirit, is delivered from all adherence to the creatures, and united to

God, whatever be his knowledge, and whatever his virtue, they are of little value: he must remain in an infant state, groveling upon earth, while he esteems anything great and good but one alone, the eternal and immutable God. The difference between the meek wisdom of an illuminated mind devoted to me, and the pompous wisdom of a critical and classical speculatist, is as incommensurate, as between the knowledge that "is from above, and cometh down from the Father of light," and that which is laboriously acquired by the efforts of human understanding.

Many are solicitous to attain to contemplation as an exalted state, who take no care to practice that abstraction which is necessary to qualify them for the enjoyment of it: for while they adhere to the objects of sense, to external services, and the signs of true wisdom, instead of the substance, rejecting the mortification of self, as of no value, they adhere to that which principally obstructs the progress to perfection.

DISCIPLE: Alas, Lord! we who have assumed the profession and character of spiritual men, know not at what our purposes aim, nor by what spirit we are led, that we exert so much labor, and feel so much solicitude about that which is external, but retire so seldom to the sacred solitude of the heart to learn what passes within us. Irresolute and impatient as we are, after a slight recollection, we rush into the world again, unacquainted with the nature and end of the actions which we pretend to examine. We heed not by what our affections are excited, nor in what they terminate; but, like those of old, "when all flesh had corrupted his way," an universal deluge of earthliness overwhelms us, and we are lost in folly, impurity, and darkness. Our inward principle being thus corrupt, it cannot but be that our actions, which flow from it, must be corrupt also; for it is only out of a pure heart that the Divine fruits of a pure life can be brought forth.

We busily inquire what a man hath done, but not from what principle he did it: we ask whether this or that man be valiant, rich, beautiful, or ingenious; whether he be a profound scholar, an elegant writer, or a fine singer: but how poor in spirit he is, how patient, how meek, how holy and resigned, we disregard as questions of no importance. Nature looks at the outward man, but grace at the inward. Nature dependeth wholly upon itself, and always errs; grace trusts wholly in God, and is never deceived.

LVIII. THE RENUNCIATION OF ANIMAL DESIRE.

CHRIST: Without a total denial of self, my son, thou canst not attain the possession of perfect liberty. All self-lovers and self-seekers are bound as in chains of adamant; full of desires, full of cares; restless wanderers in the narrow circle of sensual pleasures, perpetually seeking their own luxurious ease, and not the interests of their self-denying, crucified Saviour; but often pretending this, and erecting a fabric of hypocrisy that cannot stand; for all that is not of God must perish.

But do thou, my son, keep invariably to this short hut perfect rule: *Abandon all, and thou shalt possess all, relinquish desire, and thou shalt find rest.* Revolve this again and again in thy mind; and when thou hast transfused it into thy practice, thou wilt understand all things.

DISCIPLE: Lord! this is not the work of a single day, nor an exercise for children; for in this short precept is included the high attainments of "a perfect man in thee."

CHRIST: Start not aside, my son, nor he depressed with fear, when thou hearest of the way of the perfect; but rather be excited to walk in it, or at least, aspire after it with all the energy of desire. O that self-love was so far subdued in thee, that with pure submission thou couldst adhere to the intimations of my will, as well in the government of thy spirit as in the disposals of my providence with respect to thy outward situation! Thou wouldst then be pleasing and acceptable in my sight, and thy life would pass on in peace and joy. But thou hast still much to abandon, which must be wholly surrendered up to me before that rest which thou so earnestly seekest can be found. "I counsel thee," therefore, "to buy of me gold tried in the fire, that thou mayst be rich;" heavenly wisdom, which trampleth the earth and its enjoyments under her feet.

I have told thee that what is low and vile in human estimation is to be purchased at the expense of what is esteemed exalted and precious. What men regard as contemptible and most unworthy of thought and remembrance, is heavenly wisdom. That wisdom vaunteth not herself, nor seeketh the applause of men; and many "honor with their lips," who in their hearts renounce it.

LIX. THE INSTABILITY OF THE HEART.

CHRIST: Trust not, my son, to the ardor of a present affection; for it may soon be past, and coldness succeed. As long as thou livest in this fallen world, thou wilt, even against thy will, be subject to perpetual mutability, now joyful, and now sad: now peaceful, and now disturbed; at one time ardent in devotion, at another insensible; today diligent, tomorrow slothful; this hour serious, and the next trifling. But he that hath true wisdom, and deep experience in the spiritual life, is raised above the fluctuation of this changeable state: he regards not what he feels in himself, nor whence the wind of instability blows, but studies only that his mind may be directed to its supreme and final good. And thus, in all the various events of this changeable life, he remains unchanged and unmoved, by directing aright the eye of his intention, and fixing it solely upon me.

In most men, this eye of the intention soon waxeth dim; it is easily diverted by intervening objects of sensual good, and it is seldom free from some natural blemish of self-seeking. Thus, those Jews who went to Bethany, to the house of Martha and Mary, went not only to see and hear Jesus, but to gaze upon Lazarus, whom he had just raised from the dead. The eye of the intention, therefore, must be continually purified, till it becomes perfectly single, and, disregarding all intermediate objects of pleasure and profit, looks solely unto me.

*   *   *   *   *

[Something is wanting here in the Manuscript]

LX. THE SOUL THAT LOVES GOD ENJOYS HIM IN ALL THINGS.

DISCIPLE: Behold, thou art my God, and my all! What would I desire more? What higher happiness can I possibly enjoy? O sweet and transporting sounds! But to him only who loveth "not the world, neither the things that are in the world," but thee. My God, and my all! Enough to say, for him that understandeth; and often to say it, delightful to him that loveth!

When blessed with thy presence, all that we are and have is sweet and desirable; but in thy absence, it becomes loathsome. Thou calmest the troubled heart, and givest true peace and holy joy. Thou makest us to think well of all thy dispensations, and to praise thee in all. Without thee, the highest advantages cannot please long; for, to make them truly grateful, thy grace must be present, and they must be seasoned with the seasoning of thy own wisdom.

What bitterness becomes not sweet to him that truly tasteth thee? And to him by whom thou art not relished, what sweetness will not be bitter? The wise of this world, and those that delight in the enjoyments of the flesh, are destitute of the wisdom that enjoyeth thee; for in the world is found only vanity, and in the flesh, death. They who, by the contempt of the world, and the mortification of the flesh, truly follow thee, know that they are wise in thy wisdom; and find themselves translated from vanity to truth, from the flesh to the Spirit. These only enjoy God: and whatever is found good and delightful in the creature they refer to the praise and glory of the Creator. Infinitely great, however, is the difference between the enjoyment of the Creator, as he is in himself, and as he is discovered in imperfect creatures; of eternity, and of time; of uncreated light, and of light communicated.

O eternal light, infinitely surpassing all that thou illuminatest, let thy brightest beams descend upon my heart, and penetrate its inmost recesses! O purify, exhilarate, enlighten and enliven my spirit, that with all its powers it may adhere to thee in raptures of triumphant joy! O when will the blessed and desirable moment come, in which thou wilt satisfy me with thy presence, and be in me and to me all in all? Till this is granted me, my joy cannot be full.

Wretched creature that I am! I find the old man still living in me; he is not yet perfectly crucified, he is not yet dead. The flesh still strongly lusteth against the spirit, still kindles the rage of war, and suffers not "thy kingdom within me" to be at peace.

But do thou, O God! "who controllest the power of the sea, and stillest the raging of its waves," arise and help me! "Scatter thou those that delight in war!" O break them in pieces with thy mighty power! Show forth, I beseech thee, the wonders of thy greatness, and let thy right hand be glorified! For there is no hope nor refuge for me, but in thee, O Lord, my God!

CHRIST: As long as thou livest in this world, my son, thou canst not live secure, but wilt always have need of "the whole armor of God." Thou art encompassed with enemies, who assault thee behind and before, on the right hand and on the left; and if thou dost not defend thyself on every side with the shield of patience, thou canst not long escape some dangerous wound: if thy heart is not fixed upon me, with a true and unalterable resolution of suffering all things for my sake, thou wilt never be able to sustain the fury of the conflict, nor obtain the palm of victory. Thou must, therefore, with a lively faith, and a holy resolution of conquering all opposition, pass through the various dangers that surround thee. "To him that overcometh, I will give to eat of the hidden manna," while for the slothful and unbelieving is reserved the portion of endless misery.

If thou seekest rest in this life, how wilt thou attain to the everlasting rest of the life to come? Prepare thy heart for the exercise of many and great troubles, not for the enjoyment of continual rest: true rest is to be found, not on earth, but in heaven; not in the enjoyment of man, or any other creature, but of God. For the love of God, therefore, thou must cheerfully and patiently endure labor and sorrow, persecution, temptation, and anxiety, poverty and want, pain and sickness, detraction, reproof, humiliation, confusion, correction, and contempt. By these, the virtues of "the new man in Christ Jesus," are exercised and strengthened; these form the ornaments of his celestial crown; and for his momentary labor, I will give him eternal rest, and endless glory for transient shame.

"The sufferings of the present time are not worthy to be compared with the glory that should be revealed in us." "O wait on the Lord; be of good courage; and he shall strengthen thy heart." Distrust me not, neither depart from me; but continually devote both soul and body to my service, and my glory. "Behold, I come quickly, and my reward is with me!" and till I come, my Spirit will be thy comforter in every tribulation.

LXI. AGAINST THE FEAR OF MAN.

CHRIST: My son, fix thy heart steadfastly upon the Lord; and while conscience bears testimony to thy purity and innocence, fear not the judgment of man. It is good and blessed to suffer the false censure of human tongues; nor will the suffering itself be grievous to the poor and humble in spirit, who confideth not in himself, but in God.

The opinions and reports of men are as various as their persons, and are, therefore, entitled to little credit. Besides, it is impossible to please all: and though Paul endeavored to please all men in the Lord, and was "made all things to all;" yet, with him, it was "a very small thing to be judged of man's judgment." This faithful servant labored continually to promote the edification and salvation of men; but their unjust judgments, and cruel censures, he was not able to restrain: he therefore committed his cause to God, who knoweth all things; and sheltered himself against the false suggestions of the deceitful, and the more open reproaches of the licentious, under the guard of patience and humility: yet he sometimes found it expedient to support his character, that he might not give occasion of scandal to the weak, who are too apt from silence to infer guilt.

"Who," then, "art thou, that thou shouldst be afraid of a man that shall die, and of the son of man, that shall be made as grass, which today is, and tomorrow is cast into the oven?" Fear God, who is a "consuming fire;" and thou wilt no longer tremble at the terrors of man. What hurt can man do thee, by his most malignant censures, or his most cruel actions? He injureth himself more than he can injure thee; and whoever he be, he shall not escape the righteous judgment of God. Set God, therefore, continually before thy eyes, and strive not with the injustice of man: and though at present thou art overborne by its violence, and sufferest shame which thou hast not deserved; yet suppress thy resentment, and let not impatience obscure the luster of thy crown. Look up to me in the highest heavens, who am able to deliver thee from all evil, and will render to everyone according to his deeds.

LXII. GOD IS OUR REFUGE IN ALL DIFFICULTIES.

CHRIST: Endeavor, my son, in every place, and in every external employment and action, to be inwardly free, and master of thyself; that the business and events of life, instead of ruling over thy spirit, may be subject to it. Of all thy actions, thou must be, not the servant and slave, but the absolute lord and governor; a free and genuine Israelite, translated into the inheritance and liberty of the sons of God; who stand upon the interests of time, to contemplate the glories of eternity; who cast only a hasty glance on the transitory enjoyments of earth, and keep their eye fixed upon the permanent felicity of heaven; and who, instead of making temporal objects and interests an ultimate end, render them subservient to some purpose of piety or charity, even as they were ordained by God, the sovereign mind, who formed the stupendous fabric, in which nothing disorderly was left.

If thus, in all events, thou sufferest not thyself to be governed by appearances, nor regardest what is heard and seen with a carnal purpose; but in every difficulty and danger enterest immediately into the Tabernacle with Moses, to consult the Lord, thou shalt often receive an answer from the Divine Oracle, and return deeply instructed both in things present and things to come. And as Moses always retired to that holy place, for the determination of doubtful and disputed questions, and fled to prayer, for aid in times of danger and wickedness, so shouldst thou also enter the sacred temple of thy heart, and, on the same occasions, fervently implore the guidance and support of Divine wisdom and strength. Thou hast read, that Joshua and the children of Israel, "because they asked not counsel at the mouth of the Lord," were betrayed into a league with the Gibeonites, being deluded by fictitious piety, and giving hasty credit to deceitful words. Commit thy cause invariably to me, and I will give it a right issue in due season. Wait patiently the disposals of my providence, and thou shalt find "all things work together for thy good."

DISCIPLE: Lord, I would most willingly resign my state, present and future, to thy disposal; for my own restless solicitude and feeble reasoning serve only to perplex and torment me. O that I took no anxious thought for the events of to-morrow, but could every moment unreservedly offer up all I am to thy good pleasure!

CHRIST: Man vehemently labors for the acquisition of that which he desires; but possession defeats enjoyment, and his desire, which is restless and insatiable, is immediately turned to some new object. It is, therefore, no email advantage, to suppress desire even in inconsiderable gratifications.

Self-denial is the basis of spiritual perfection; and he that truly denies himself, is arrived at a state of great freedom and safety. The old enemy, however, whose nature is most repugnant to that which is most good never remits his diligence; but night and day forms the most dangerous ambuscades, if peradventure, in some moment of false security, he may surprise and captivate the unwary soul. I have, therefore, cautioned thee, continually to "watch and pray, that thou enter not into temptation."

LXIII. MAN HAS NOTHING WHEREIN TO GLORY.

DISCIPLE: "Lord, what is man, that thou art mindful of him; and the son of man, that thou visitest him?" What, indeed, is he, and what hath he done, that thou shouldst bestow upon him thy Holy Spirit.

What cause have I to complain, O Lord, when thou withdrawest thy presence, and leavest me to myself? Or how can I remonstrate, though my most importunate requests are not granted? This only I can truly think and say: "Lord, I can do nothing, and have nothing: there is no good dwelling in me that I can call my own, but I am poor and destitute in all respects, and always tending to nothing; and if I were not quickened by thy Spirit, I should immediately become insensible as death."

"Thou, O Lord, art always the same, and shalt endure forever." Thou art always righteous and good; with righteousness and goodness governing the whole universe, and ordering all its concerns by the counsels of infinite wisdom. But I, who of myself am more inclined to evil than to good, never continue in holiness and peace; I am changeable as the events of time that pass over me; am tossed upon every wave of affliction, and driven by every gust of passion. Yet, Lord, I shall find stability when thou reachest forth thy helping hand; for thou canst so firmly strengthen and support me that my heart shall no longer change with the various changes of this fallen life, but being wholly turned to thee, shall in thee find supreme and everlasting rest.

Wherefore, if I could but perfectly abandon all human consolation, either from a purer love and devotion to thee, or from the pressure of some severe distress, which, when all other dependence was found ineffectual, might compel me to seek after thee; then might I hope to receive more abundant measures of confirming grace, and to rejoice in new and inconceivable consolation from thy Holy Spirit.

Thanks are due to thee, O Lord, from whom all good proceeds, whenever my state is better than I have reason to expect. I am an inconstant and feeble man, and vanity and nothing before thee. What have I then to glory in? And why do I desire to be esteemed and admired? Is it not for nothing? And that, surely, is most vain. Vain glory is not only the vainest of all vanities, but a direful evil, that draws away the soul from true glory, and robs it of the grace of heaven: for while man labors to please himself, he labors to displease thee; while he sighs for the perishing laurels of the world, he loses the unfading crown of thy righteousness.

Truly glory and holy joy are to be found only in thee; and man should rejoice in thy name, not in the splendor of his own imaginary virtues, and delight in no creature but for thy sake. Praised, therefore, be thy name, not mine; magnified be thy power, not my work! Yea, forever blessed be thy holy name; but, to me let no praise be given! Thou art my glory, and the joy of my heart! In thee will I glory, and in thee rejoice, all the day long; and "of myself I will not glory, but in mine infirmities!"

Let men "seek glory one of another;" I will seek that "glory which cometh only from thee," my God. For all human glory, all temporal honor, all worldly grandeur, is vanity and folly; and vanishes like darkness before the splendor of thy eternal majesty. O my truth, my mercy, my God! O holy and blessed Trinity! Fountain of life, light, and love! To thee alone be praise, honor, power, and glory ascribed, through the endless ages of eternity! Amen.

LXIV. TEMPORAL HONOR AND COMFORT.

CHRIST: Grieve not, my son, when others are honored and exalted, and thou art despised and debased. Lift up thy heart to me in heaven, and thou wilt not be disturbed by the contempt of men on earth.

DISCIPLE: Lord, I am surrounded with darkness, and easily betrayed into a vain conceit of my own dignity and importance; but when I behold myself by thy light, I know that no creature has done me wrong; and, therefore, surely I have no cause to complain of thee. On the contrary, because I have heinously and repeatedly sinned against thee, all creatures may justly treat me as an enemy, and make war against me. To me only shame and confusion of face are due; but to thee, praise, and honor, and glory. And, till I am perfectly willing to be despised and forsaken of all creatures, as that nothing which in myself I truly am, I know that my restless spirit cannot possibly be established in peace, nor illuminated by truth, nor brought into union with thee.

CHRIST: Son, if thou sufferest even a conformity of sentiments and manners, and the reciprocations of friendship, to render thy peace dependent upon any human being, thou wilt always be unsettled and distressed; but if thou continually seekest after me the ever-living and abiding truth as the supreme object of thy faith and love, the loss of a friend will be no affliction, whether it happens by falsehood or by death. The affections of friendship must spring from the love of me; and it is for my sake alone that any person should be dear in the present life, as there is no goodness in man but what he receives immediately from me. Without me, therefore, friendship has neither worth nor stability; nor can there be any mutual ardors of pure and genuine love but what I inspire.

As far as the distinct improvement and perfection of thy own spirit is concerned, thou shouldst so mortify personal affections and attachments as to make them hold a subordinate place in thy heart. The soul draws near to God only in proportion as it withdraws from earthly comfort. With so much higher exaltation doth it ascend to him, as, with deeper conviction of its inherent darkness and impurity, it descends into itself, and becomes viler and more contemptible in its own sight. But he that claims any goodness in himself bars the entrance to the grace of God; for the Holy Spirit chooses, for the seat of his influence, a contrite and humble heart.

If thou wert brought to a true sense of thy own nothingness, and emptied of all selfish and earthly affections, I would, surely, with the treasures of grace, "come unto thee and make my abode with thee:" but while thou fondly gazest upon, and pursuest the creature, thou turnest from the presence and sight of the Creator. Learn, therefore, for the love of the Creator, to subdue this earth-born love of the creature, and thou wilt be qualified to receive the light of eternal truth. It matters not how inconsiderable the object of pursuit is in itself: while it is vehemently loved, and continually regarded, it corrupts the soul, and keeps it at an infinite distance from its supreme good.

LXV. A CAUTION AGAINST VAIN PHILOSOPHY.

CHRIST: Be not captivated, my son, by the subtlety and elegance of human compositions; for "the kingdom of God is not in word, but in power." Attend only to the truths of my word, which enlighten the understanding, and inflame the heart; which excite compunction, and pour forth the balm of true consolation. Read my word, not for the reputation of critical skill and controversial wisdom, but to learn how to mortify thy evil passions: a knowledge of infinitely more importance than the solution of all the abstruse questions that have perplexed men's minds, and divided their opinions.

When, however, thou hast meekly and diligently read my word, still thou must also have recourse to me. I am he that teacheth man knowledge, and giveth that light and understanding to the prayerful which no human instruction can communicate. He who listeneth to my voice shall soon become wise, and be renewed in the spirit of truth. But, woe be to them who, instead of turning to me to learn my will, devote their time and labor to vain theories of human speculation!

I am he that exalteth the humble and simple mind, and imparteth to it, in a short time, such a perception of eternal truth, as it could not acquire by a life of study in the schools of men. I teach not like men, with the clamor of uncertain words, or the confusion of opposite opinions; or with the strife of formal disputation, in which victory is more contended for than truth: I teach in still and soft whispers, to relinquish earth, and seek after heaven; to relinquish carnal and temporal enjoyments, and sigh for spiritual and eternal; to shun honor, and to bear contempt; to place all hope and dependence upon me, to desire nothing besides me; and, above all in heaven and on earth, most ardently to love me.

LXVI. OF THE PROFESSIONS AND CENSURES OF MEN.

CHRIST: It is expedient for thee, my son, to be ignorant of many things; and to consider thyself as "crucified to the world, and the world to thee." Like one deaf, let what is said pass by thee unnoticed, that thou mayst keep thy thoughts fixed on "the things that belong unto thy peace." It is better to turn away from all that produces perplexity and disturbance, and to leave everyone in the enjoyment of his own opinion, than to be held in subjection by contentious arguments. If thou wert truly "reconciled to God," and didst regard only his unerring judgment, thou wouldst easily bear the disgrace of yielding up the victory in the debates of men.

DISCIPLE: Do thou, O Lord, "give me help from trouble; for vain is the help of man!" How often have I failed of support where I thought myself sure of it; and how often found it where I had least reason to expect it! Vain and deceitful, therefore, is all trust in man; but the salvation of the righteous, O Lord, is in thee! Blessed, therefore, be thy holy name, O Lord, my God, in all things that befall us! We are weak and unstable creatures, easily deceived, and suddenly changed.

Where is the man that, by his own most prudent care and watchful circumspection, is always able to avoid the mazes of error and the disorders of sin? But he, O Lord, that puts his whole confidence in thee, and in singleness of heart seeks thee alone, will not easily be betrayed into either: and though he chance to fall into some unexpected trouble, and be ever so deeply involved in it; yet thy merciful hand will soon deliver him from it, or thy powerful consolations support him in it, for thou wilt not utterly forsake him that putteth his whole trust in thee. A comforter, that will continue faithful in all the distresses of his friend, is rarely to be found among the children of men; but thou, Lord, thou art most faithful at all times, and in all events; and there is none like unto thee in heaven or earth. O how Divinely wise must be that holy soul, who could say, "My heart is firmly established, for it is rooted in Christ!" If this was my state, I should no longer tremble at the threats of wrath, nor be disturbed by the calumnies of envy.

Who can foresee future events? Who can guard against future evil? If those evils that are foreseen often hurt us, we cannot but be grievously wounded by those that are unforeseen. But, wretched creature that I am, why did I not provide more wisely for the security of my peace? Why have I given such easy credit to men like myself, who are all destitute both of wisdom and power, though many think us, and call us angels? Whom ought I to have believed? Whom, Lord, but thee! Who art the truth, that can neither deceive nor be deceived! But "all men are liars;" so frail and inconstant, so prone to deceive in the use of words, that hasty credit is never to be given, even to those declarations that wear the appearance of truth.

How wisely hast thou warned us, O Lord, to "beware of men!" How justly said, that "a man's enemies are those of his own house!" and how kindly commanded us to withhold belief, when it is said, "Lo, Christ is here:" or, "Lo, he is there!" I have learned these truths, not only from thy word, but at the expense of peace; and I pray that they may more increase the caution than manifest the folly of my future conduct.

With the most solemn injunctions of secrecy, one says to me, "Be wary, be faithful; and let what I tell thee be securely locked up in thy own breast:" and while I hold my peace, and believe the secret inviolate, this man, unable to keep the silence he had imposed, to the next person he meets, betrays both himself and me, and goes his way to repeat the same folly. From such false and imprudent spirits, protect me, O Lord! that I may neither be deceived by their insincerity, nor imitate their practices. Give truth and faithfulness to my lips, and remove far from me a deceitful tongue; that I may not do that to another, which I am unwilling another should do to me.

How peaceful and blessed a state must that man enjoy, who takes no notice of the opinions and actions of others; who does not indiscriminately believe, nor wantonly report, everything he hears; who, instead of unbosoming himself to all he meets, continually looks up to thee, the only Searcher of the heart; and who is not "carried about with every wind of doctrine," but studies and desires only, that everything, both within and without him, may be directed and accomplished according to thy will!

It is of great importance, Lord, for the preservation and improvement of thy heavenly gift, to shun the notice of the world; and, instead of cultivating attainments that attract admiration and applause, to aspire, with continual ardor, after inward purity, and a perfect elevation of the heart to thee. How often has the growth of holiness been checked, by its being too hastily made known, and too highly commended! And how greatly hath it flourished, in that humble state of silence and obscurity, so desirable in the present life, which is one scene of temptation, one continual warfare!

LXVII. CONFIDENCE IN THE RIGHTEOUS JUDGMENT OF GOD.

CHRIST: Place all thy hope, my son, in my mercy, and stand firm against false accusations: for what are words, but puffs of air, that are of short continuance, and leave no impression? If thou art guilty, resolve to make the accusation an occasion of amendment; if thou art innocent, submit to it willingly, and bear it patiently, for my sake. It is surely a little matter for thee, who hast not endured the lasting pain of cruel stripes, sometimes to bear the light buffeting of transient words. Could affliction make so deep an impression upon thy heart, if thou wert not still carnal, and didst not set too high a value upon the favor of men? Thou art afraid of being despised; and, therefore, canst not bear reprehension, but laborest to conceal thy iniquities, or palliate them by excuses. Examine now the state of thy heart, and confess, that a vain desire of pleasing men is the governing principle of thy actions: for whilst thou refusest to be brought to shame, and be buffeted for thy faults, it is evident that thou art not truly humbled, not yet "crucified to the world, nor the world to thee."

Give ear to my word, and thou wilt not be moved by ten thousand opprobrious words of men. Consider, if everything was said against thee that the most extravagant malignity can suggest, what hurt could it possibly do thee, if thou only lettest it pass without resentment? Could it pluck from thy head a single hair? He that liveth not in my presence manifested in his heart, is disturbed by the lightest breath of human censure; but he that referreth his cause to me shall be free from the fear of man. I am the sole judge of man's actions, and the discerner of his most secret thoughts: I know the nature, the cause, and the effect of every injury; and make a just estimate of the wrong that is done by the injurious, and sustained by the sufferer. The word of reproach came forth from me; it was uttered by my permission, "that the thoughts of many hearts might be revealed:" for though the innocent and the guilty shall be judged in the face of the whole world, at the last day, yet it is my will to try both beforehand, by a secret judgment, unknown to all but myself.

The testimony of man is fallible, partial, and changeable; my judgment is true, righteous, and permanent as my own being. To me, therefore, thou must refer thy cause in all human accusation, and not trust to the blind and partial determinations of thy own mind. The righteous should never be moved by whatever befalls him, knowing that it comes from the hand of God. Therefore, if thou art falsely accused, be not cast down; or if justly defended, do not triumph: for consider that "I, the Lord, search the heart and try the reins;" that I judge not, as man judgeth, by deceitful appearances; and that, therefore, what is highly esteemed by him, is often abomination in my sight.

DISCIPLE: O Lord God, the consciousness of innocence is not sufficient to sustain me under the pressure of false accusation: be thou, therefore, O most righteous and most merciful Judge, the Omniscient and Almighty, my confidence and my strength!

Thou knowest what I know not; thou knowest my secret faults, and how justly I deserve continual reprehension. I ought, therefore, whether I think I deserve it or not, to humble myself under every reproof of man, and bear it with meekness. O pardon me, as often as I have not done this; and mercifully bestow upon me the grace of more perfect submission!

It is surely much safer for me to depend for deliverance from all my evil, upon the free and boundless mercy manifested in thy sacred humanity; than presuming upon particular instances of imperfect righteousness, to justify myself before men, when there is so much evil in me that escapes the notice of my own mind. And though in many instances my conscience condemns me not, yet am I not therefore justified; because, without the merciful gifts of righteousness which is in thee, no one living can be justified in thy sight.

LXVIII. THE HOPE OF ETERNAL LIFE.

CHRIST: My son, neither let the labors which thou hast voluntarily undertaken for my sake, break thy spirit, nor the afflictions that come upon thee in the course of my providence, utterly cast thee down. I am an abundant recompense, above all comprehension and all hope. Thou shalt not long labor here, nor groan under the pressure of continual trouble. Wait patiently the accomplishment of my will, and thou shalt see a speedy end of all evil: the hour will quickly come when labor and sorrow shall cease; for everything is inconsiderable and short that passeth away in the current of time.

What thou hast to do, therefore, do with thy might. Labor faithfully in my vineyard; I myself will be thy reward. Write, read, sing my praises, bewail thy own sins, pray in the spirit, and with patient resolution bear all afflictions: eternal life is worthy not only of such watchful diligence, but of the severest conflicts.

The day is coming, fixed by my unalterable decree, when, instead of the vicissitudes of day and night, and joy and sorrow, there shall be uninterrupted light, infinite splendor, unchangeable peace, and everlasting rest. Then thou wilt no longer say, "Who shall deliver me from the body of this death?" nor exclaim, "Woe is me, that my pilgrimage is prolonged!" for death shall be swallowed up in victory, and "the corruptible will have put on incorruption." Then "all tears shall be wiped away from thy eyes," and all sorrow taken from thy heart; and thou shalt enjoy perpetual delight in the lovely society of angels, and "the spirits of the just made perfect."

O, was it possible for thee to behold the unfading brightness of those crowns which the blessed wear in heaven; and with what triumphant glory they, whom the world once despised, and thought unworthy even of life itself, are now invested; verily, thou wouldst humble thyself to the dust, and be resigned to thy inferiority. Instead of sighing for the perpetual enjoyment of the pleasures of this life, thou wouldst rejoice in suffering all its afflictions for the sake of God, and wouldst count it great gain to be despised and rejected as nothing among men.

If a true sense of these astonishing glories, which are offered thee as the object of thy faith and hope, had entered into the depths of thy heart, couldst thou utter one complaint of the evil of thy state? Is any labor too painful to be undertaken, any affliction too severe to be sustained, for eternal life? Is the gain or loss of the kingdom of God an alternative of no importance? Lift up thy thoughts and thy desires, therefore, continually to heaven. Behold, all who have taken up the cross, and followed me, the Captain of their salvation, in resisting and conquering the evil of this fallen state, now rejoice securely, and shall abide with me forever in the kingdom of my Father!

DISCIPLE: O most blessed mansion of the heavenly Jerusalem! O most effulgent day of eternity, which night obscureth not, but the supreme truth continually enlighteneth! A day of perennial peace and joy, incapable of change or intermission! It shineth now in the full splendor of perpetual light to the blessed; but to the poor pilgrims on earth, it appeareth only at a great distance, and "through a glass darkly." The redeemed sons of heaven triumph in the perception of the joys of this eternal day, while the distressed sons of Eve lament the irksomeness of days teeming with distress and anguish. How is man defiled with sins, agitated with passions, disquieted with fears, tortured with cares, embarrassed with refinements, deluded with vanities, encompassed with errors, worn out with labors, vexed with temptations, enervated with pleasures, and tormented with want!

O when will these various evils be no more? When shall I be delivered from the slavery of sin? When, O Lord, shall my thoughts and desires center and be fixed in thee alone? When shall I regain my native liberty? O, when will peace return, and be established; peace from the troubles of the world, and the disorders of sinful passions; universal peace, incapable of interruption; that "peace which passeth all understanding?" When, O most merciful Jesus! when shall I stand in pure abstraction from all inferior good to gaze upon thee, and contemplate the wonders of redeeming love? When wilt thou be to me all in all? O, when shall I dwell with thee in that kingdom which thou hast prepared for thy beloved before the foundations of the world?

Soften, I beseech thee, the rigor of my banishment, assuage the violence of my sorrow! For my soul thirsteth after thee; and all that the world offers for my comfort would but add more weight to the burden that oppresses me. I long, O Lord, to enjoy thee truly, and would fain rise to a constant adherence to heavenly objects; but the power of earthly objects, operating upon my unmortified passions, keeps me down. My mind labors to be superior to the good and evil of this animal life, but my body constrains it to be subject to them. And thus, "wretched man that I am," while the spirit is always tending to heaven, and the flesh to earth, my heart is the seat of incessant war, and I am a burden to myself!

O, what do I suffer, when raising my soul to thee, a crowd of carnal images suddenly rush upon me, and intercept my flight. "O my God, be not far from me! Put not away thy servant in anger! Cast forth thy lightning, and scatter" the illusions of the enemy; "shoot out thine arrows, and destroy" his power! Call in my wandering thoughts and desires, and unite them to thyself; efface the impressions of worldly objects; give me power to cast away immediately the imaginations of wickedness. O Eternal Truth, establish me in thyself, that no blast of vanity may have power to move me! O immaculate purity, enter the temple of my heart, and let all that is unholy be driven from thy presence!

In merciful compassion to my infirmity, pardon me, O Lord, my wandering thoughts in prayer. I confess that my distractions are great and frequent; and, instead of being present in spirit where I stand or kneel, I am carried to various places, just as my roving thoughts lead me. Thou, O Truth, hast expressly declared, that "where the treasure is, there will the heart be also." And accordingly I find, in the various revolutions of my changeable heart, that when I love heaven, I take pleasure in meditating on heavenly enjoyments; when I love the world, I think with delight on its advantages, and with sorrow on its troubles; when I love the flesh, my imagination wanders among its various pleasures; when I love the Spirit, my faculties are with holy joy devoted to spiritual exercises. Whatever I chiefly love, of that I delight chiefly to hear and speak; and I carry home with me the diversified images of it, even to my most secret retirement.

LXIX. THE DESIRE AND PROMISE OF ETERNAL LIFE.

CHRIST: My son, when thou perceivest the heaven-born desire of eternal life rising within thee, open thy heart wide, and with all the eagerness of hunger receive this holy inspiration. Without any mixture of complacency and self-admiration, let all thy thanks and praise be faithfully rendered to the sovereign goodness which so mercifully dealeth with thee, so condescendingly visitest thee, so fervently exciteth thee, and so powerfully raiseth thee up, lest, by the propensity of thy own nature, thou shouldst be immovably fixed to the earth. For this new principle of life within thee is not the production of thy own reasoning and thy own efforts, but is the fruit of Divine grace and redeeming love, to lead thee on to holiness, to feed thee with humility, to sustain thee in all conflicts with sinful nature, and to enable thee to adhere to me with all thy heart.

The fire of devotion is often ardent in thy heart; but the flame ascends not without smoke. Thy desires, while they burn for the enjoyment of heaven, are sullied with the dark vapors of carnal affection; and that which is so earnestly sought from God is not sought wholly and purely for his honor. That cannot be pure which is mixed with self-interest. Make not, therefore, thy own delight and advantage, but my will and honor, the ground and measure of all thy requests; for if thou judgest according to truth, thou wilt cheerfully submit to my appointment, and always prefer the accomplishment of my will to the gratification of thy desires.

I know thy desire, and thy groaning is not hid from me. Thou wouldst this moment be admitted into the glorious liberty of the sons of God; thou longest for the immediate possession of the celestial mansions, and the unfading pleasures of the heavenly Canaan: but thy hour is not yet come. Thou wishest now to be filled with the sovereign good, but thou art not yet capable of enjoying it.

Thou must be proved upon earth, and exercised with various troubles. Some measures of consolation shall be imparted to animate and sustain thee in thy conflicts; but the plenitude of peace and joy is reserved for the future world. "Be strong, and of good courage," therefore, in doing and in suffering; for thou must now "put on the new man," with new perceptions, will, and desires.

While this important change is making, thou wilt often be obliged to relinquish thy own will, and do that which thou dislikest, and forbear that which thou choosest. Often the designs of others will succeed, and thy own prove abortive; what others say shall be listened to with eager attention, but what thou sayest shall either not be heard, or rejected with disdain; others shall ask once, and receive; thou shalt ask often, and not obtain; the tongue of fame shall speak long and loud of the accomplishments of others, and be utterly silent of thine! And others shall be advanced to stations of wealth and honor, while thou art passed by, as unworthy of trust, or incapable of service. At such trials, nature will be greatly offended and grieved; and it will require a severe struggle to suppress resentment: yet much benefit will be derived from a meek and silent submission; for by such the servant of the Lord proves his fidelity in denying himself, and subduing his corrupt appetites and passions.

If thou wilt consider the speedy end of all these trials, and the everlasting peace and blessedness that will succeed, they will then, so far from being occasions of disquietude and distress, furnish the most comfortable encouragements to persevering patience. In exchange for that small portion of corrupt and selfish will which thou hast freely forsaken in this world, thou shalt always have thy will in heaven: there, whatever thou wiliest, thou shalt find; and whatever thou desirest, thou shalt possess: there thou shalt enjoy all good without the fear of losing any part. Thy will being always the same with mine, shall desire nothing private and personal, nothing out of me, nothing but what I myself desire: thou shalt meet with no resistance, no accusation, no contradiction, no obstruction; but all good shall be present at once to satisfy the largest wishes of thy heart. There, for transient shame patiently endured, I will give immortal honor; "the garment of praise for the spirit of heaviness;" and for the lowermost seat an everlasting throne. There the fruits of obedience shall flourish, the labor of penitence rejoice, and the cheerfulness of subjection receive a crown of glory.

LXX. A DESOLATE SPIRIT COMMITTING ITSELF TO GOD.

DISCIPLE: O Lord God, holy Father, be thou blessed now and forever! For whatever thou willest, is done; and all that thou wiliest, is good. Let thy servant rejoice, not in himself, nor in any other creature, but in thee; for thou only art the object of true joy: thou, O Lord, art my hope and exaltation, my righteousness and crown of glory! What good do I possess, which I have not received from thee, as the free and unmerited gift of redeeming love? All is thine, whatever has been done for me, or given to me

"I am poor and afflicted from my youth up and sometimes my soul is sorrowful, even unto death; and sometimes is filled with consternation and terror at the evils that threaten to overwhelm me. But I long, O Lord, for the blessings of peace; I earnestly implore the peace of thy children, who are sustained by thee in the light of thy countenance. Shouldst thou bestow peace; shouldst thou pour forth the treasures of heavenly joy; the soul of thy servant shall be tuned to harmony, and devoutly celebrate thy praise. But if thou still withholdest thy enlivening presence, I cannot "run the way of thy commandments;" but must smite upon my bosom, because it is not with me as it was once, "when thy lamp shone upon my head."

O Father, ever to be praised, now is the hour of thy servant's trial! O merciful

Father, ever to be loved, it is well that thy servant should suffer something for thy sake! O Father, infinitely wise, and ever to be adored, that hour is come, which thou didst foreknow from all eternity, in which thy servant shall be oppressed and enfeebled in his outward man, that his inward man may live to thee forever! It is necessary I should be disgraced, humbled, and brought to nothing, in the sight of men; should be broken with sufferings, and worn down with infirmities; that I may be prepared to rise again in the splendor of the new and everlasting day, and be glorified with thee in heaven!

It is thy peculiar favor to him whom thou hast condescended to choose for thy friend, to let him suffer in this world, in testimony of his fidelity and love: and be the affliction ever so great; and however often, and by whatever hand it is administered, it comes from the counsels of thy infinite wisdom, and is under the direction of thy merciful providence; for without thee nothing is done upon the face of the earth. Therefore, "it is good for me, O Lord, that I should be afflicted, that I may learn thy statutes," and utterly cast from me all self-confidence and self-exaltation. It is good for me, that "shame should cover my face:" that in seeking comfort, I may have recourse, not to men, but to thee; that I may learn to adore in silence thy unsearchable judgments.

I give thee thanks, O Father of mercies, that thou hast not spared the evil that is in me; but hast humbled sinful nature by severe chastisements, inflicting pains, and accumulating sorrows, both from within and from without; and of all in heaven and on earth, there is none that can bring me comfort but thou, O Lord my God, the sovereign physician of diseased souls; "who woundest and healest, who bringest down to the grave, and raisest up again!" Thy chastisement is upon me, let thy rod teach me wisdom!

Behold, dear Father, I am in thy hands, and bow myself under the rod of thy correction! O teach my untractable spirit a ready compliance with thy righteous will! Make me thy holy and humble disciple, as thou hast often done others, that I may cheerfully obey every intimation of thy good pleasure! To thy merciful discipline I commend all that I am, and bless thee, that thou hast not reserved me for the awful and penal chastisements of the future world. Thou knowest the whole extent of being, and all its parts; and no thought or desire passeth in the heart of man, that is hidden from thy sight. From all eternity, thou knowest the events of time; thou knowest what is most expedient for my advancement in holiness, and how effectually tribulation contributeth to wear away the rust of corruption. Do with me, therefore, O Lord, according to thy own will.

Grant, O Lord, that from this hour, I may know only that which is worthy to be known; that I may love only that which is truly lovely; that I may praise only that which chiefly pleaseth thee; and that I may esteem what thou esteemest, and despise that which is contemptible in thy sight! Suffer me no longer to judge by the imperfect perception of my own senses, or of the senses of men ignorant like myself; but enable me to judge both of visible and invisible things, by the Spirit of Truth; and, above all, to know and to obey thy will. How great an instance of this fallibility of judgment, is the glory that is given and received among men! For none is made great by the voice of human praise. When men extol each other, the cheat imposes upon the cheat, the vain flatters the vain, the blind leads the blind, the weak supports the weak.

LXXI. WE MUST ACCOUNT OURSELVES RATHER WORTHY OF AFFLICTION THAN COMFORT.

CHRIST: Thou hast not been able, my son, to continue in the uninterrupted enjoyment of spiritual fervor, nor always to stand upon the heights of pure contemplation, through the influence of that evil nature into which thou art fallen. Thou must sometimes feel thy poverty and weakness, though with shame and regret. As long as thou art united to an earthly body, thy days will often be full of heaviness, and thy heart of sorrow. Unable to escape from flesh and blood, thou must still feel the severity of its restraints, and groan under the power of those carnal appetites that interrupt the exercises of the Spirit, and intercept thy views of heaven.

In such seasons of weakness and sorrow, it is necessary for thee to be the more earnest in external exercises, and seek relief in the diligent practice of common duties; with assured confidence expecting my return, and with meek patience bearing this state of banishment to darkness and desolation, till I visit thee again, and deliver thee from all thy distress. Then I will make thee forget past sufferings, in the enjoyment of profound peace; I will so fully open to thy mind the Divine truths contained in my written word, that thou shalt begin with "an enlarged heart to run the way of my commandments," and in the joyful anticipation of the heavenly life, thou shalt feel and confess, that "the sufferings of the present time are not worthy to be compared with the glory that shall be revealed in thee."

DISCIPLE: Lord, I am unworthy, not only of the superior comforts, but of the least visitations of thy Spirit; and, therefore, thou dealest righteously with me, when thou leavest me to my own poverty and wretchedness. Though, from the anguish of my soul, "rivers of tears" were to "flow day and night," still thou wouldst deal righteously with me, if thou still shouldst withdraw thy consolations: for I am worthy only of stripes and afflictions, because I have frequently and obstinately resisted thy will, and in many things have heinously offended. From a faithful retrospect of my past life, I cannot plead the least title to the smallest favors, but "thou, O Lord, art a God full of compassion, and plenteous in mercy."

What am I, O Lord, and what have I done, that thou shouldst bestow upon me any consolation? So far from being able to recollect the least goodness proceeding from myself, I have been always prone to evil, and insensible and sluggish under the sanctifying influences of thy grace. Should I say otherwise, thou wouldst stand in judgment against me, and there is none that would be able to support my cause. My sins are so numerous and aggravated, that they have exposed me to everlasting wrath; much more have they rendered me unworthy of the society of thy faithful servants, from which I deserve to be driven, as an object of universal scorn and contempt.

But, oppressed with guilt, and filled with confusion as I am, what shall I say? I have no power to utter more than this: I have sinned, O Lord, "against thee only have I sinned. Have mercy upon me, according to thy loving-kindness; and according to the multitude of thy tender mercies, blot out all my transgressions" Bear with me a little while, that I may truly bewail my corruption and misery, "before I go to the land of darkness," that is covered with the shadow of death. And from a sinner laden with such aggravated guilt, what other reparation dost thou desire for his transgressions, and what other is he capable of, but a heart broken with holy sorrow and humbled to the dust?

In true contrition and humiliation, the hope of pardon hath its birth: there the troubled conscience is set at rest: man is delivered from the wrath to come; and

God and the penitent soul meet together with a holy kiss. The humble sorrow of a broken and a contrite heart is thy chosen sacrifice, O Lord, infinitely more fragrant than clouds of burning incense: it is the precious ointment, with which thou desirest to have thy holy feet anointed. A broken and a contrite heart, thou never didst, nor ever will despise.

LXXII. THE GRACE OF GOD COMPORTS NOT WITH THE LOVE OF THE WORLD.

CHRIST: Son, my grace, which is infinitely pure, like the fountain from whence it flows, cannot unite with the love of sensual pleasure, and worldly enjoyment. If, therefore, thou desirest to receive this heavenly gift, thou must banish from thy heart every affection that obstructs its entrance. Choose a place of undisturbed privacy for thy resort; delight in retirement and solitude; and, instead of wasting thy invaluable moments in the vain and unprofitable conversations of men, devote them to prayer and holy intercourse with God, which will increase compunction, and purify thy conscience. Thou must wean thy heart from all human consolation and dependence; and be able to forsake even thy most intimate associate and dearest friend. This duty, and the ground of it, I have already taught thee by my apostle Peter, who earnestly beseeches my faithful followers to consider themselves, as they truly are—"strangers and pilgrims" in the world; and, in that character, to abstain from the indulgence of earthly and carnal affections "which war against the soul."

With what confidence and peace shall that man, in the hour of his dissolution, look on death, whom no personal affection or worldly interest binds down to the present life! When self is once overcome, the conquest of every other evil will be easy. This is the true victory; this the glorious triumph of the new man! And he, whose sensual appetite is kept in continual subjection to his spirit, and his spirit in continual subjection to my will, he is this mighty conqueror of himself, and the lord of the whole world.

If, with holy ambition, thou desirest to ascend this height of perfection, thou must set out with a resolved will, and first lay the ax to the root, that self may be cut off. From self-love, as the corrupt stock, are derived the numerous branches of that evil which forms the trials of man in his struggles for redemption; and when this stock is plucked up by the roots, holiness and peace will be implanted in its room, and flourish forever with unfading verdure. But how few labor for this extirpation! How few seek to obtain the Divine life, which can only rise from the death of self! And thus men lie bound in the complicated chains of animal passions, unwilling, and, therefore, unable to rise above the selfish enjoyments of flesh and blood.

LXXIII. THE DIFFERENT OPERATIONS OF NATURE AND GRACE.

CHRIST: My son, observe, with watchful attention, the motions of nature and grace; for though infinitely different, they are yet so subtle and intricate as not always to be distinguished but by an illuminated and sanctified spirit. Men invariably desire the possession of good; and some good is always pretended as the constant motive of their words and actions; and, therefore, many are deluded by an appearance of good, when the reality is wholly wanting.

Nature is crafty: she allures, ensnares, deceives, and continually designs her own gratification as her ultimate end. But grace walks in simplicity and truth; "abstains from all appearance of evil;" pretends no fallacious views; but acteth from the pure love of God, in whom she rests as her supreme and final good.

Nature abhors the death of self; will not be restrained, will not be conquered, will not be subordinate, but reluctantly obeys when obedience is unavoidable. Grace, on the contrary, is bent on self-mortification; continually resists the sensual appetite; seeks occasion of subjection; longs to be subdued, and even uses not the liberty she possesses: loves to be restrained by the rules of strict discipline; and has no desire for the exercise of authority and dominion.

Nature is always laboring for her own interest; and, in her intercourse with others, considers only what advantages she can secure for herself: but grace regards that most which is most subservient to the common good.

Nature, as her chief distinction, is fond of receiving honor and applause; grace faithfully ascribes all honor and praise to God, as his unalienable right.

Nature dreads ignominy and contempt, and cannot bear them even in the cause of truth; but grace rejoices to suffer reproach for the name of Jesus.

Nature courts idleness and rest; grace shuns idleness as the nurse of sin, and embraces labor as the duty and blessing of life.

Nature delights in the splendor of dress; hates and despises what is coarse and vulgar, and wearies imagination in the contrivance of ornament. But grace, instead of decorating the body, spontaneously puts on plain and humble garments, nor refuses even those that are disagreeable to the flesh, ill-fashioned, and decayed.

Nature regards only the good and evil of this temporal world; is elated with success, depressed by disappointment, and kindled into wrath by the least breath of reproach. But grace adheres not to the enjoyments of time and sense; is neither moved by loss or gain, nor incensed by the bitterest invectives, but lives in the hope of eternal life.

Nature continually seeks after those treasures which may not only be corrupted by moth and rust, and stolen by thieves, but which are in themselves perishing and evanescent. Grace lays up treasures in heaven, where nothing perisheth, nothing fadeth; and "where neither moth nor rust do corrupt, nor thieves break through and steal."

Nature is covetous; grasps at peculiarity of possession, and greedily takes what she hates to give away. Grace is benevolent and bountiful to all; regards property as really belonging to God; is content with the necessary supports of life; and esteems it "more blessed to give than to receive."

Nature is strongly disposed to the enjoyment of the creatures, to the gratification of sensual desire, and to incessant wandering from place to place in quest of new delight. Grace is continually drawn after God and goodness; she restrains the desire of wandering, and even for shame declines being seen in places of public resort.

Nature, in the depths of distress, seeks all comfort from that which produces animal delight: grace has no comfort but in God; and leaving below this visible world, seeks rest only in the enjoyment of the sovereign good.

Nature always acts upon principles of self-interest; does nothing good for its own sake; but for every benefit expects either a present recompense, or such an establishment in the favor and approbation of men as will secure a future return of some superior good; and besides expecting to receive back in kind, desires to have her services and gifts highly esteemed and applauded. Grace, for the highest offices of charity and bounty, expects no recompense from men, but continually looks up to God as her exceeding great reward: has no temporal interests to excite anxiety, for she desires no greater share of the possessions of time than is necessary to sustain her in her progress to eternity.

Nature exults in the extensive interest of numerous relations and friends; glories in dignity of station and splendor of descent; fawns upon the powerful; caresses the rich; and, with partial commendation, applauds those most that are most like herself. But grace loves her enemies, and, therefore, counts not the number of her friends; values not the splendor of station, and the nobility of birth, but as they are dignified by superior virtue: favors the poor rather than the rich; compassionates the innocent more than the powerful, rejoices with him that obeys the truth, not with the hypocrite; and continually exhorts even the good, not only to "covet earnestly the best gifts," but in "a more excellent way," by Divine charity, to become like the Son of God.

Nature, when she feels her want and misery, quickly and bitterly complains: grace bears, with meekness and patience, all the poverty and wretchedness of this fallen state.

Nature refers all excellence to herself; argues and contends for her own wisdom and her own goodness: but grace, conscious of Divine origin, refers all the excellence she has to God; does not arrogantly presume upon her own wisdom and goodness, but ascribes neither goodness nor wisdom to herself; contends not for a preference of her own opinion to the opinion of another; but in her search after truth, submits every thought and sentiment to the correction and guidance of infinite wisdom.

Nature is fond of deep researches, and with eager curiosity listens to that which is new and strange: affects to be busy about the rectitude of public opinions, and pretends to demonstrate truth by sensible experiment; desires to be known as the guardian of men's minds from the imposition of religious error; and pursues those inquiries most that most attract admiration and applause. But grace does not follow the cry of novelty, nor is captivated by subjects of curious and refined speculation: knowing that the lust of vain wisdom is derived from the old stock of human corruption; and that all that is new in this sublunary world, is no more than the varied forms of its own vanity and misery: she restrains the busy activity of the senses; suppresses vain complacency, shuns the ostentation of human learning; conceals, under the veil of humility, the gifts and graces of the Holy Spirit; and, in every observation and discovery, seeks only the fruits of holiness, and the praise and honor of God. She desires not that herself and her own wisdom and goodness may he proclaimed and celebrated, but that God may he blessed and glorified in all his gifts, who with pure love bestoweth all that is possessed both by angels and men.

Such is the transcendency of grace to nature! She is the offspring of the light of heaven, the immediate gift of God, the peculiar distinction of the elect, and the pledge of eternal happiness; by whose power the soul is raised from earth to heaven, and from carnal transformed to spiritual. The more, therefore, our sinful nature is suppressed and subdued, the more grace lives and triumphs; and, by superadded communications of light and strength, "the inward man is, day by day," more and more "renewed after the image of him that created him."

DISCIPLE: O Lord, my God, who didst create me after thy Divine image, from which I am now fallen; mercifully bestow upon me the grace which thou hast represented as so necessary to my restoration, that my depraved nature, which is always tending to sin and perdition, may be totally subdued! I feel in myself a "law of sin warring against the law of my mind, and bringing me into captivity" to sensual and malignant passions, which I cannot resist, till thy Holy Spirit kindles in my heart another fire.

I have need of the continual operation of his sanctifying power, to overcome all the workings of revolted nature, which is disposed to evil from its birth. It fell in Adam, and fallen, descended from him to all mankind, who have increased its obliquity by voluntary and habitual sin.

From this ground it is, O, my God! that "I delight in thy law after the inward man," convinced that "the commandment is holy, just, and good," condemning all evil, and warning against the practice of it; "but with the flesh I serve the law of sin," and submit to the rigorous tyranny of sensual appetite, instead of the mild government of thy Spirit: from this it is, that "to will is present with me; but how to perform that which is good, I find not." From this it is that I form purposes of holiness; but, upon the trial of my strength to accomplish them, am driven back by the least difficulty. Though I know the path that leads to the summit of perfection, and clearly discern by what steps it is to be ascended, yet laden and oppressed with the burden of my corruption, I am unable to make any progress in it. How indispensably necessary, therefore, is thy grace, O Lord, by whose power alone every good work must be begun, continued, and perfected! Without that power, I can do nothing that is acceptable to thee; but with it, I can do all things.

O grace essentially Divine! Thou hast all merit within thyself, and givest to the endowments of nature all their value; for what is beauty, or strength, or wit, or learning, or eloquence, in the sight of God, where grace does not dwell? The endowments of nature are common to the evil and the good; but the ornaments of grace are the peculiar marks of the elect, and all that are distinguished by them shall inherit eternal life. The chief grace is charity; without which, neither the gift of prophecy, nor the power of working miracles, nor the knowledge of the profoundest mysteries, are of any profit; not even faith, and hope, and that zeal which bestoweth all its possessions to feed the poor, and giveth the body to be burned, are acceptable to thee, O God, without charity.

Come, then, O Lamb of God! Thou who makest the poor in spirit rich in goodness, and the rich in goodness poor in spirit; O come, descend into my soul, and fill it with the light and comfort of thy blessed presence, lest it faint and perish in the darkness and barrenness of its fallen state!

O God of all grace and consolation! That I may find grace in thy sight is the sum of my requests; for thy grace in Jesus Christ is abundantly sufficient to supply all my wants, if I were even destitute of everything that nature loves and covets. Though I am tempted and troubled on every side; "yea, though I walk through the valley of the shadow of death;" yet, while thy grace is with me, "I will fear no evil." She is my strength, my counsel, and my defense; mightier than all enemies, and wiser than all the wise. She is the revealer of truth, the mistress of holy discipline, the sanctifier of the heart, the comforter of affliction, the banisher of fear and sorrow, the nurse of devotion, the parent of contrition. Without her quickening power, I should soon become an unfruitful and withered branch upon the tree of life, fit only to be cast away, or thrown into the fire. Grant, therefore, O most merciful Lord, that thy grace may abide with me continually.

LXXIV. THE IMPORTANCE OF SELF-DENIAL.

CHRIST: The more thou forsakest thyself, my son, the nearer wilt thou approach to me. I would have thee, therefore, without the least reluctance or murmur, make an unreserved sacrifice of thyself to my will. Follow me; "I am the way, the truth, and the life." Only by the way which I have opened, canst thou attain to Paradise. Without the truth which I teach, thou canst not know the way; and without the life which I impart, thou canst not obey the truth. I am the way thou must go, the truth thou must believe, and the life thou must desire. I am the invariable and perfect way; the supreme and infallible truth; the blessed, the uncreated, and endless life. In me "thou shalt know the truth, and the truth shall make thee free."

This I have already declared in the sacred record of my precepts; and have also told thee, that, "if thou wilt enter into life, thou must keep the commandments;" if thou wilt know the truth, thou must "continue in my word;" if thou wilt be my disciple; thou must "deny thyself;" if thou wilt keep thyself for eternal life, thou must hate[32] thy temporal life; if thou wouldst be exalted in heaven, thou must humble thyself on earth; and if thou wilt reign with me, thou must take up thy cross, and suffer with me: for the path of light and glory is found only by the servants of the cross, who, "through much tribulation must enter into the kingdom of God."

DISCIPLE: Lord Jesus! Thy way is narrow and painful, and despised by the world: do thou enable me to walk in it, and with meekness and patience bear contempt: "for the disciple is not above his master, nor the servant above his lord." Let me be continually exercised in the study and imitation of thy most holy life, in which all perfection and blessedness is centered. Whatever else I hear, or read, or think of, gives me neither instruction nor delight.

CHRIST: Son, "if thou knowest these things, happy art thou if thou doest them." "He that hath my commandments, and keepeth them, he it is that loveth me: and I will love him, and will manifest myself to him," and make him to sit down with me in the kingdom of my Father.

DISCIPLE: Lord, I beseech thee, that this gracious promise may be accomplished in thy servant! I receive the cross from thee; and by the strength of that Almighty hand which laid it upon me, I will bear it even unto death.

The new principle begotten in thy disciples imposes continual restraint on natural appetites and passions, but without such control they would not follow the light that leads to Paradise. O suffer me not to look back with a partial and selfish fondness for the good of this world, however specious; lest I incur the dreadful disqualification for "the inheritance of thy kingdom."

Come, my beloved brethren, let us take courage, and hand in hand pursue our journey in the path of life: Jesus will be with us, for Jesus' sake we have taken up the cross; and, for Jesus' sake, we will persist in bearing it: He, who is our captain and our guide, will be our strength and our support. Behold our King, who will fight our battles, leads the way! Let us resolutely follow, undismayed by terrors; let us choose death, rather than stain our glory by deserting the cross.

---

32   The word hate is here used in its Scriptural sense, which is not always *to bear ill will*. Very often it means, *to love far less in comparison*. Thus must we hate father and mother, year, and our own life also in comparison with Christ. Luke xiv. 26.—Ed.

LXXV. AGAINST EXTRAVAGANT DEJECTION.

CHRIST: Humility and patience under adversity are more acceptable to me, my son, than joy and fervor when all is prosperous and peaceful.

Why art thou offended and grieved at every little injury from men; when, if it were much greater, it ought to be borne without emotion? As fast as such evils arise, let their influence be banished from thy mind: they are not new; thou hast met with many, and, if thy life be long, shalt meet with many more.

When adversity stands not in thy path, thou dost boast thy fortitude; and can give excellent counsel to others, whom thou expectest to derive strength from thy exhortations: but no sooner do the same evils that oppressed them turn upon thyself, than fortitude forsakes thee, and thou art destitute both of counsel and strength. O let the frequent instances of the power which the lightest evils have over thee, keep thee continually mindful of thy great frailty. No evil, however, is permitted to befall thee, but what may be made productive of a much greater good.

When thou meetest with injury from the violence or treachery of men, exert all thy resolution to drive the thoughts of it from thy heart: but if it toucheth thee too sensibly to be soon buried in forgetfulness, let it neither depress nor vex thee; and if thou canst not bear it cheerfully, at least bear it patiently. If any censure that is uttered against thee be too severe and cruel to be heard in silence, suppress thy indignation before it burst into flame; and suffer no expression of impatience and resentment to escape thy lips, that may give occasion of scandal to the weak. The storm that is thus raised within thee will soon subside; and the wounds thy heart has received from the arrows of reproach, shall be healed by the influence of restoring grace. I live forever; ready to help thee upon all occasions, and to bestow abundant consolation upon thee, if thou devoutly callest upon me for it.

Keep thy mind then calm, and girded for severer conflicts. Because thou art often strongly tempted, and deeply troubled, thou must not think that all is lost. Thou art man, not God; a spirit fallen, not a pure angel. How canst thou expect to continue in one unchangeable state of enjoyment? Give up thyself wholly to my mercy: I am he who comforteth all that mourn; and raiseth to a participation of Divine strength all that are truly sensible of their weakness.

DISCIPLE: Thy words, O Lord, distill as dew, and are "sweeter than honey, or the honeycomb." What would become of me, in the midst of so much darkness, corruption, and misery, without thy Holy Spirit to illuminate, sanctify, and comfort me? I will not regard what, nor how much I suffer, if I can but be made capable of enjoying thee, my supreme and only good! Be mindful of me, O most merciful God! Grant me a safe passage through this vale of sin and sorrow, and in the true path conduct me to thy heavenly kingdom! Amen.

LXXVI. AGAINST THE PRESUMPTUOUS INQUIRIES OF REASON.

CHRIST: Forbear to reason, my son, upon deep and mysterious subjects, especially the secret judgments of God. Ask not, Why this man is forsaken, and that distinguished by a profusion of grace: why one is so deeply humbled, and another so eminently exalted. These things surpass the limits of human understanding; nor can the deepest reasoning investigate the proceedings of the Most High. When, therefore, such questions are either suggested by the enemy, or proposed by the vain curiosity of men, answer in the words of the royal prophet, "Righteous art thou, O Lord! and just are thy judgments. The judgments of the Lord are true, and righteous altogether." My judgments are to be feared, not discussed; for they are incomprehensible to every understanding but my own.

Forbear also to inquire and dispute concerning the preeminence of apostles and martyrs; who is the most holy, and who the greatest in the kingdom of heaven. These questions produce the strife of unprofitable debate, and nourish presumption and vain glory.

I am he who formed all the saints; I gave them grace, I have exalted them to glory: I conferred the peculiar excellence which distinguishes each, "preventing[33] him with the blessings of goodness." I knew my beloved before the birth of time; and chose those out of the world, who had not chosen me: I called them by the free determination of sovereign goodness, atoned for them by my sufferings, drew them with the cords of love, and led them in safety through various temptations. I poured upon them the consolations of my Spirit, and crowned the patience which I enabled them to exercise. I own the last as well as the first, and embrace every one with inestimable love. I alone, who am always to be blessed and praised, am to be "admired and glorified in all my saints."

They are now raised far above the influence of unholy nature, which is ever tending to the love of self; and are passed into my love, in which they dwell with unutterable peace and joy. This love no power is able to alter or suppress; for it is the inextinguishable fire of their own life, "delivered from the bondage of darkness," and restored to its union with eternal truth.

Beware, my son, of being led by vain curiosity to "search the things that are above thy strength:" and let all thy faculties be employed in that only needful and important inquiry, how thou thyself mayst be found in the kingdom of heaven, though in the least and lowest place. What does knowledge avail, unless it makes us more humble, and excite greater ardor to glorify my name? He who, in constant attention to the state of his own soul, laments the multitude and enormity of his sins, and the small number and imperfection of his virtues; and when he thinks on glorified spirits, thinks only how exceedingly remote he is from the perfection which they have attained; is more acceptable to me, than he who employs his time and thoughts in considering and disputing about the different degrees of excellence and glory that distinguish the particular members of that illustrious assembly. It is infinitely more useful, and more safe, with tears and prayers to implore grace to imitate the great examples they have left; than to labor, by fruitless inquiries into their state, to know what no human understanding is able to comprehend.

Men should be content with the imperfect knowledge of their fallen state, and suppress their vain curiosity, and refrain from their vainer disputes. Happy spirits glory not in any personal excellence; for they arrogate no good themselves, but ascribe all to me, who with infinite liberality have freely given them whatever they possess. The consummation of their honor and happiness, is found in their boundless love of God, and their joyful celebration of his praise. The more exalted their state is, the more humble is their spirit; and, therefore, it is written, that the four and twenty elders, who were seated round the throne of heaven, "cast their crowns before the throne, and fell down before him that sat on the throne; and worshiped him that liveth forever and ever."

Many solicitously inquire into the subject of degrees in glory who utterly

---

33   The only sense of the word *prevent* in the Scriptures, is, *to put, or go before.*—Ed.

neglect the infinitely more important inquiry, whether they themselves are likely to be numbered there, even among the least.

When the disciples, whom I had chosen to attend my ministry upon earth, inquired who should be "the greatest in the kingdom of heaven," it was answered, "Except ye be converted, and become as little children, ye shall not enter into the kingdom of heaven. But whosoever shall humble himself as a little child, the same is greatest in the kingdom of heaven." Woe be to them, therefore, who cherish the pride of human attainments; for the gate of the kingdom of heaven is too low to give them entrance! "Woe unto them that are rich, who say they are increased in (mental) riches, and have need of nothing, for they have received their consolation;" and while the poor enter into the kingdom, they shall stand weeping and wailing without! But rejoice, ye humble, and leap for joy, ye poor in spirit! For while ye continue in the truth that has made you what ye are, "yours is the kingdom of God!"

LXXVII. HOPE AND CONFIDENCE TO BE PLACED IN GOD ALONE.

DISCIPLE: Lord, what is my confidence in this life, and what my comfort in the possession and enjoyment of all things under heaven? Is it not thee alone, O my God, whose mercies are without number, and without measure? Where hath it been well with me, if thou wert absent? I had rather be naked, hungry, and despised with thee, than abound in honor, wealth, and pleasure, without thee: would rather choose, with thee, to wander, and have no place "where to lay my head," than, without thee, to possess a throne in heaven. Where thou art, there is heaven; and death and hell are only there where thou art not. Thou art the desire of my soul; and to thee my sighs and groans, my cries and prayers, shall continually ascend. There is none that is able to deliver me from my necessities; none in whose power and goodness I can trust, but thee, O my God! Thou art my refuge and my hope in every distress; my powerful Comforter, and most faithful friend!

Though thou permittest me to be exposed to the trial of various troubles, yet dost thou mercifully superintend the conflict, and direct the event to my supreme and everlasting good: "for whom thou lovest, thou chastenest; and scourgest every son whom thou receivest." In this awful probation, thou art not less to be loved and praised than when thou fillest my soul with heavenly consolations. Thou alone, therefore, O Lord my God, art my hope and sanctuary; with thee I leave all my tribulation and anguish, and resign the beginning, continuance, and end of every trouble, to thy blessed will.

Wherever I look for support and consolation out of thee, I find nothing but weakness and distress: and if thou dost not revive, strengthen, and illuminate, deliver, and preserve me, the friendship of mankind can give no consolation, the strength of the mighty bring no support, the counsel of the wise, and the labors of the learned, impart no instruction, the treasures of the earth purchase no deliverance, and the most secret places afford no protection. All persons and things that seem to promise peace and happiness are in themselves vanity and nothing, and subvert the hope that is built upon them: but thou art the supreme, essential, and final good; the perfection of life, light, and love!

"Unto thee do I lift up mine eyes, O thou that dwellest in the heavens!" In thee, the Father of mercies, I place all my confidence! O illuminate and sanctify my soul with the influence of thy Holy Spirit; that being delivered from all the darkness and impurity of its alienated life, it may become the living temple of thy holy presence, the seat of thy eternal glory! In the immensity of thy goodness, O Lord, and "in the multitude of thy tender mercies, turn unto me," and hear the prayer of thy poor servant, who hast wandered far from thee into the region of the shadow of death. O protect and keep my soul amid the innumerable evils which this corruptible life is always bringing forth; and by the perpetual guidance of thy grace, lead me in the narrow path of holiness to the realms of everlasting light and peace. Amen.

Printed in Great Britain
by Amazon

59307064R00067